LAKE COUNTY
WINE GUIDE

"Wine is bottled poetry"

ROBERT LOUIS STEVENSON

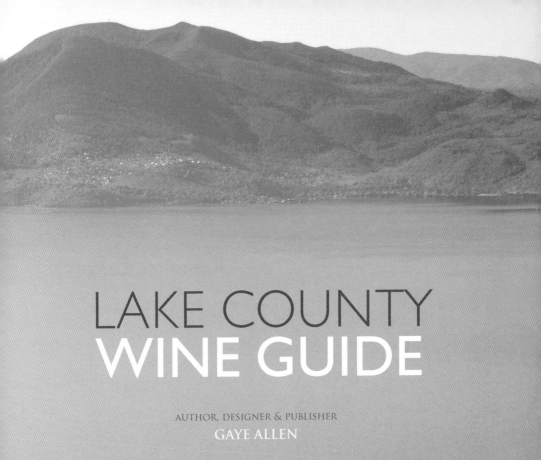

LAKE COUNTY
WINE GUIDE

AUTHOR, DESIGNER & PUBLISHER
GAYE ALLEN

MANAGING EDITOR
KAREN MacDOUGALL

ASSOCIATE EDITOR
KAREN SLOOTEN

ACKNOWLEDGMENTS

In this brand new new edition of the *Lake County Wine Guide*, Karen MacDougall has very graciously stepped in to manage the daily rigours of chasing down, compiling, and presenting this new information in a clear and insightful way. For this second edition, Karen has double checked many of the facts from the first edition, and has lent a keen new editorial eye to the existing book. Karen Slooten, who made the first edition possible, kindly has helped with reading and proofing the guide. I must also thank Wilda Shock for generously reading the book so thoroughly and giving me some helpful editorial comments which we have embraced and incorporated.

Other kind original readers were Sheila O'Brien, Beverly Hill, Christopher Rowland, Lynne & Bernie Butcher, Toni & Phil Scully, Diane Henderson, Myron & Marilyn Holdenried, Madelene Lyon, Else Ahlmann, and Jared Hendricks.

Particular thanks to Debra Sommerfield, President of the Lake County Wine Grape Commission, who has given appreciated help, support, and advice (over the years!). Thank you to Terry Dereniuck and Maria Brunn, past and present, Executive Directors of the Lake County Winery Association. Many other specialists have also been kind enough to read parts of the text and give expert advice, including Greg Giusti, Harry and Roberta Lyons, Kris Eutenier, Glen McGourty, Randy Krag, Paul Zellman, Gregory Graham, Peter Molnar, and Michael Wood.

A big thank you also to Alan Flora for his kind and generous help with the maps.

A very special thank you to Linda Lake, the former Curator at the Historic Courthouse Museum, who provided quite invaluable assistance to the history and geology sections of this book, and also to her knowledgeable and helpful colleagues Dwain Goforth and Teresa Rushing, my sincere thanks.

PICTURE CREDITS

Thank you to the wineries who supplied pictures for this guide, and many thanks to the following individuals and organizations: The Historic Courthouse Museum archive collection, the Schoolhouse Museum archive collection, and the Lake County Historical Society for generously supplying all the historical pictures in this book: Aerial Archives p.16, 47, 49, 50; Rocco Ceselin p.16 (middle); Else Ahlmann p. 11 (bottom left), 40 (right/top),124 (bottom), 94-95; Lake County Winegrape Commission/ Hannah Henry p.12,14, 41 (top), 48, 51; LCWGC p.43 (top); Madelene Lyon p. 36; Jim Warren p.36 (top right); Molly Hartz p. 40 (top); National Portrait Gallery p. 78; Bob Colin p.43 (bottom) 84, 85; Lisa Teso p.117; Karen Pavone p.130,131; Casey Carney p.128 (top left); Dirk Slooten p.129 (bottom), Gigi Stahl p.129 (top right). Blaise Bahara p.125 (top), JIm Robello p.127 (top & middle) Back cover: Dirk Slooten (top) Nathan de Hart (second and third from top), also P.127 &134 bottom, and cover photo.

PUBLISHER'S NOTE

Despite the wonderful army of people who have generously assisted me in compiling this book, I take full responsibilty (and offer humble apologies) for any errors. Please send any corrections/suggestions you may have to: Gaye Allen at Meadowlark Publishing. To order books please email:

gaye@meadowlarkpublishing.com

© Meadowlark Publishing.

Welcome to a Unique Wine Region

Winemaking in Lake County is not at all new. The wine industry stretches back to Gold Rush days when early settlers began to produce wines, drawing from a wealth of different winemaking traditions. By the late nineteenth century the county had sizeable wineries and thousands of acres under vine. The early wine industry attracted serious investment and considerable critical acclaim. When Prohibition stalled things, the county developed a pear and walnut industry that is still thriving today and is a delightful feature of wine touring in the county. In the mid 1960s a handful of forward-looking local farmers planted winegrapes again. Today, just fifty years later, the wine industry has matured and is booming once again, offering a remarkable selection of world-class wines.

The high altitude and unique volcanic soils of this region offer some distinct advantages to the winemaker. The stronger UV light found at high elevations produces grape with thicker skins and more intensely concentrated fruit.

The hot summer days followed by cooling from the lake and colder evening temperatures are key to the quality and sheer variety of grapes that thrive here. An exciting new generation of winemakers has been drawn to the unique Lake County terroir. It is their passion for the art of winemaking that is celebrated here.

Only in Lake County can you sip wine on the side of a volcano, look out over an ancient lake, and watch a herd of deer, Tule Elk, or maybe even a Bald Eagle pass by. This is real, relaxed, rural wine country where sheep roam through the vines, and where an extraordinary collection of excellent hand-crafted wines, served by the winemaker or friendly locals, awaits you. With the 100-mile perimeter lake and over 600,000 acres of public lands to explore, there are many adventures beyond wine tasting to enjoy.

Wherever your Lake County travels take you,

Cheers! *Gaye Allen*

Contents

The Formation of Lake County's Unique Mountain Wine Region

California's North Coast AVA

FORMING THE COASTAL RANGES

140 million years ago California began to form to the west of the Sier Nevada mountains due to the effects of Plate Tectonics. The oceanic Farallo plate, moving east, collided with and slipped under the continental North American plate, creating a subductio zone. This period of mountain buildir created a succession of ridges, each further to the west and parallel to th coastline. These are now called the Coastal Ranges. Franciscan "complex basement rocks are found throughou the North Coast. These rocks formee as sea bed deposits were piled up at the entrance to the subduction zone, and then underwent massive change involving heating, stretching, faulting compression, known as metamorphis These ranges were later uplifted and weathered over millennia creating th rolling (wine) valleys we see today.

California produces 85% percent of all wines made in America today: over 238 million cases. Over half of all the AVAs (American Viticultural Areas) in America are also here. An AVA is a clearly defined wine growing area with specific unifying elements, such as geology, topography, climate, even history. A 10°F difference in latitude between north and south in the "Golden State" allows 100 different grape varietals to find their ideal terroir. Mark Twain may not have said, "The coldest winter I ever spent was summer in San Francisco," as many in the SF Bay Area will cite, but it certainly is true that latitude alone is not the only indicator of climate. Viticulturists in the North Coast AVA like to see some cooling of the vines in the heat of the summer to help manage fruit quality. Marine influences to the west of the AVA offer sea breezes and fog that rolls into inland valleys. Lake County, located in the northeast of this AVA, has other methods for cooling things down. At the heart of the county, Clear Lake, with its 100-mile perimeter, pulses cooling breezes over surrounding vineyards. The region's high elevation (1,300-3,000 ft.) is also very important, as summer daytime temperatures of over 90°F often drop to 50°F at night. Higher altitudes also give a stronger UV light, which produces thicker skinned grapes (which is where a lot of the color and flavor live). The North Coast AVA is one of the most prestigious wine regions in the world. Over 800 wineries have identified this area as a "sweet spot" for quality winemaking, producing the highest priced winegrapes in America. Lake County wineries sit within the North Coast AVA. A further seven AVAs or "sub-appellations" exclusive to the county are producing wines with some unique characteristics (see Lake County AVAs on page 45).

30 million years ago the Farallon plate had mostly subducted, leaving a small section—the Juan de Fuca/Gorda Plate The Pacific Plate that replaced it did n collide with the North American Plate, but slowly slid northwards against it, creating the San Andreas Fault system Between 3-5 million years ago this sliding motion caused the land to the east of the fault to uplift, creating the Coastal Ranges. The Mendocino Triple Junction is where these 3 plates (above meet, and volcanic activity linked to it has moved progressively north. It is responsible for creating the Clear Lake Volcanic Field about 2 million years ag

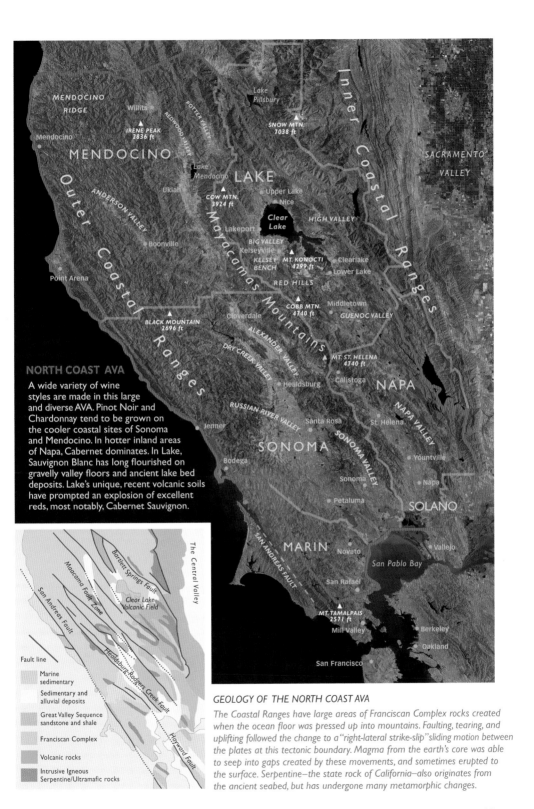

MENDOCINO RIDGE
Willits
IRENE PEAK 2836 ft
Mendocino
Lake Pillsbury
SNOW MTN. 7038 ft
Inner Coastal Ranges
SACRAMENTO VALLEY
MENDOCINO
ANDERSON VALLEY
Lake Mendocino
Ukiah
LAKE
COW MTN. 3924 ft
Upper Lake
Nice
Clear Lake
HIGH VALLEY
Outer Coastal Ranges
Boonville
Lakeport
BIG VALLEY
Kelseyville
KELSEY BENCH
MT. KONOCTI 4299 ft
Clearlake
Lower Lake
Point Arena
Mayacamas Mountains
RED HILLS
BLACK MOUNTAIN 2696 ft
COBB MTN. 4740 ft
Middletown
GUENOC VALLEY
Cloverdale
ALEXANDER VALLEY
DRY CREEK VALLEY
MT. ST. HELENA 4740 ft
Healdsburg
Calistoga
NAPA
NORTH COAST AVA

A wide variety of wine styles are made in this large and diverse AVA. Pinot Noir and Chardonnay tend to be grown on the cooler coastal sites of Sonoma and Mendocino. In hotter inland areas of Napa, Cabernet dominates. In Lake, Sauvignon Blanc has long flourished on gravelly valley floors and ancient lake bed deposits. Lake's unique, recent volcanic soils have prompted an explosion of excellent reds, most notably, Cabernet Sauvignon.

RUSSIAN RIVER VALLEY
Jenner
Santa Rosa
St. Helena
NAPA VALLEY
SONOMA
SONOMA VALLEY
Yountville
Bodega
Sonoma
Napa
Petaluma
SOLANO

The Central Valley
Bartlett Springs Fault
Mayacama Fault Zone
Clear Lake Volcanic Field
San Andreas Fault
Healdsburg-Rodgers Creek Fault
Hayward Fault

Fault line

Marine sedimentary

Sedimentary and alluvial deposits

Great Valley Sequence sandstone and shale

Franciscan Complex

Volcanic rocks

Intrusive Igneous Serpentine/Ultramafic rocks

SAN ANDREAS FAULT
MARIN
Novato
San Pablo Bay
Vallejo
San Rafael
MT. TAMALPAIS 2571 ft
Mill Valley
Berkeley
Oakland
San Francisco

GEOLOGY OF THE NORTH COAST AVA

The Coastal Ranges have large areas of Franciscan Complex rocks created when the ocean floor was pressed up into mountains. Faulting, tearing, and uplifting followed the change to a "right-lateral strike-slip" sliding motion between the plates at this tectonic boundary. Magma from the earth's core was able to seep into gaps created by these movements, and sometimes erupted to the surface. Serpentine—the state rock of California—also originates from the ancient seabed, but has undergone many metamorphic changes.

Clear Lake: Spectacular, Ancient, Unique

Clear Lake is the largest natural freshwater lake in California. It was formed as the result of powerful tectonic movements linked to the northern passage of the Mendocino Triple Junction, the leading edge of the San Andreas fault system. Five million years ago, forces that were uplifting the Coastal Ranges exerted great associated compression, heat, and faulting. In some areas, like Clear Lake, the land was stretched or pulled apart creating big depressions known as "Structural Basins." Clear Lake is formed by such tectonic activity. The Clear Lake Volcanic Field, which is still active today, began about 2 million years ago. Geologists are still debating exactly how old the lake is and how it developed, but the initial depression is likely to have formed about 2 million years ago. The Cache Formation lakebed deposits just to the east of the present lake position are up to 3 million years old. Recent core samples (some 600 feet deep) paint a much clearer picture of the last half a million years (right). That this ancient lake has survived for so long–without filling in as most freshwater lakes do–is the result of a unique geological factor. It is thought that the underlying rocks of the lakebed are down-faulting at the same rate that new sediment enters the lake, thus creating a balance which prevents Clear Lake from silting up. The lake is warm enough to swim in from April to October, and is an extremely popular destination for fishermen.

A EUTROPHIC LAKE

Clear Lake is shallow and warm (average depth 26 feet). It is eutrophic, which means it is very nutrient rich. This is good in that it supports a healthy food chain from algae to fish to birds. The lake is home to many big catfish and largemouth bass and is said to be the bass fishing capital of the west. The abundance of fish is also an important factor in attracting the impresssive 319 species of birds that are found by birdwatchers in the county. Between 1900 and 1920, in the Rodman Slough and Robinson Lake areas to the northwest, levees were constructed and the land was drained to create new farmland. Today, 50% of the water that flows into the lake still comes through Rodman Slough. In recent years it has been recognized that these former wetlands perform an important filtering function to the nutrient-rich waters that enter the lake. Plans are now in place through efforts of the Lake County Land Trust and others to restore these important wetland filters. Clear Lake is one of the most studied geological basins in California.

Geological History of Clear Lake

The lake is very unusual in that its drainage channel has changed direction a number of times in its development. When the lake was first formed it drained into the Sacramento River basin to the east via Cache Creek. Then as the result of volcanic activity, it changed to drain into the Russian River basin to the northwest via Cold Creek. A giant landslide in the Blue Lakes area about 10,000 years ago, however, caused it to re-flow back towards the Sacramento River again via Cache Creek.

THE LAKE TODAY This shape of the lake has probably remained much the same for the last 10,000 years. Scotts, Middle, Adobe and Kelsey are the main creeks that feed it.

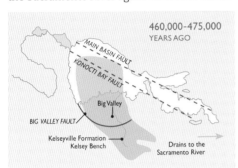

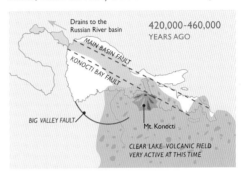

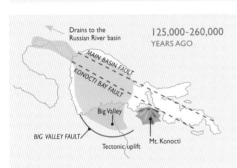

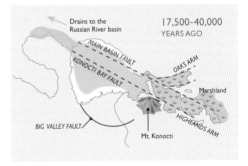

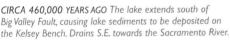

CIRCA 460,000 YEARS AGO The lake extends south of Big Valley Fault, causing lake sediments to be deposited on the Kelsey Bench. Drains S.E. towards the Sacramento River.

CIRCA 420,000 YEARS AGO Clear Lake Volcanic Field is active, and the lake shrinks to a narrow channel confined by northern fault lines. Drains N.W. to the Russian River.

CIRCA 125,000 YEARS AGO Again, the lake extends south but is contained by the Big Valley Fault, probably as the result of Kelsey Bench becoming uplifted by tectonic activity.

CIRCA 17,500 YEARS AGO Faults develop in the Oaks & Highlands arms. Lack of marine fossils suggest the area was more of a marsh; it still drains N.W. to the Russian River.

CIRCA 10,000 YEARS AGO A large landslide to the north (near Blue Lakes) blocks the N.W. exit of the lake. The lake rises and cuts a new channel to the S.W. again and also turns the Oaks and Highlands arms into part of the lake as it is today.

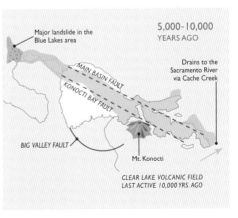

Lake County's Very Recent Volcanic Past

The Clear Lake Volcanic Field was formed 2-3 million years ago when magma from the earth's core flowed into a space opened up by powerful tectonic activity. The large 8.7-mile diameter, 18-mile deep magma chamber sits just 4.3 miles below ground. Although it is still officially considered active, it last erupted well over 10,000 years ago. Today, tourism linked to hot springs resorts and the world's largest geothermal power steam field make good use of the heat deep below ground. Various types of volcanic activity have created a dramatic and fascinating landscape, offering many geological surprises and many rich Native American legends. Mount Konocti, visible across the county, guards the lake. It is 4,299 feet high, created by repeated eruptions, making it a "stratovolcano." The multiple vents in the sides of the volcano offer hikers many different peaks from which to take in breathtaking views. The mountain itself may breathe; it is certainly scientifically possible that a system of hollow caverns and a deep vertical shaft may be inside. Hikers report unexpected rushes of air on the mountain. Kayakers in south-easterly bays of the lake encounter warm currents of bubbling water from underwater volcanic vents. Rock hunters can find Lake County diamonds and obsidian rock in areas of recent volcanic activity. For the wine lover the best news is that this extraordinary series of volcanic eruptions, lava flows and fields of volcanic ash have left behind the rocks and minerals to produce some extraordinary wines. In the Red Hills AVA, winemakers have chosen volcanic names for their local wines such as "Obsidian Ridge," "Magma Red," and "Cinder Cone."

LAKE COUNTY DIAMONDS

These sought-after gems are found across Lake County where volcanic soils are prominent. They are also called "Moon Tears," from a local Native American legend in which the moon, forced to part from a young Pomo chieftain she loved, wept these gems as tears. Some rocks have a slight pink color or occasionally a light lavender hue. With a (mohs scale) hardness rating of 7.5-8 (diamonds are 10) they also cut glass. They are a clear form of quartz (silicon dioxide) created in volcanic lava. Not having the same crystal structure of alpha quartz, they are called beta quartz. Metaphysically these "crystals" are believed to relieve sadness. Like diamonds, they can be professsionally cut and faceted. The Historic Courthouse Museum in Lakeport has some very fine examples.

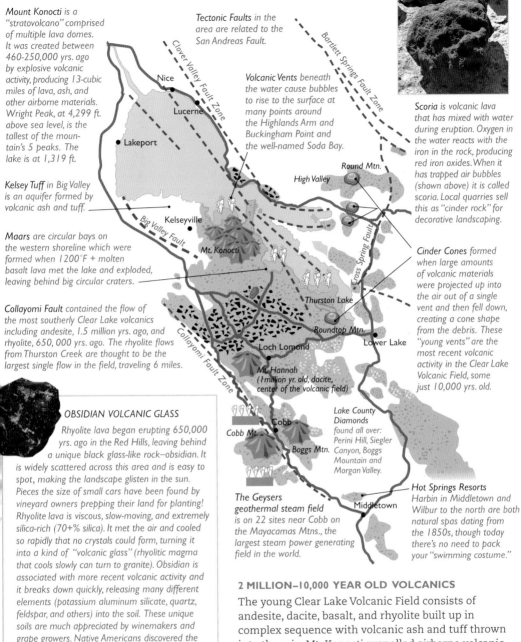

Mount Konocti is a "stratovolcano" comprised of multiple lava domes. It was created between 460-250,000 yrs. ago by explosive volcanic activity, producing 13-cubic miles of lava, ash, and other airborne materials. Wright Peak, at 4,299 ft. above sea level, is the tallest of the mountain's 5 peaks. The lake is at 1,319 ft.

Kelsey Tuff in Big Valley is an aquifer formed by volcanic ash and tuff.

Maars are circular bays on the western shoreline which were formed when 1200˚F + molten basalt lava met the lake and exploded, leaving behind big circular craters.

Collayomi Fault contained the flow of the most southerly Clear Lake volcanics including andesite, 1.5 million yrs. ago, and rhyolite, 650, 000 yrs. ago. The rhyolite flows from Thurston Creek are thought to be the largest single flow in the field, traveling 6 miles.

Tectonic Faults in the area are related to the San Andreas Fault.

Volcanic Vents beneath the water cause bubbles to rise to the surface at many points around the Highlands Arm and Buckingham Point and the well-named Soda Bay.

Scoria is volcanic lava that has mixed with water during eruption. Oxygen in the water reacts with the iron in the rock, producing red iron oxides. When it has trapped air bubbles (shown above) it is called scoria. Local quarries sell this as "cinder rock" for decorative landscaping.

Cinder Cones formed when large amounts of volcanic materials were projected up into the air out of a single vent and then fell down, creating a cone shape from the debris. These "young vents" are the most recent volcanic activity in the Clear Lake Volcanic Field, some just 10,000 yrs. old.

Map labels: Nice, Lucerne, Lakeport, Clover Valley Fault Zone, Bartlett Springs Fault Zone, Round Mtn., High Valley, Kelseyville, Big Valley Fault, Cross Spring Fault, Mt. Konocti, Thurston Lake, Collayomi Fault Zone, Roundtop Mtn., Loch Lomond, Lower Lake, Mt. Hannah (1 million yr. old, dacite, center of the volcanic field), Cobb, Cobb Mt., Boggs Mtn., Middletown

Lake County Diamonds found all over: Perini Hill, Siegler Canyon, Boggs Mountain and Morgan Valley.

The Geysers geothermal steam field is on 22 sites near Cobb on the Mayacamas Mtns., the largest steam power generating field in the world.

Hot Springs Resorts Harbin in Middletown and Wilbur to the north are both natural spas dating from the 1850s, though today there's no need to pack your "swimming costume."

OBSIDIAN VOLCANIC GLASS

Rhyolite lava began erupting 650,000 yrs. ago in the Red Hills, leaving behind a unique black glass-like rock–obsidian. It is widely scattered across this area and is easy to spot, making the landscape glisten in the sun. Pieces the size of small cars have been found by vineyard owners prepping their land for planting! Rhyolite lava is viscous, slow-moving, and extremely silica-rich (70+% silica). It met the air and cooled so rapidly that no crystals could form, turning it into a kind of "volcanic glass" (rhyolitic magma that cools slowly can turn to granite). Obsidian is associated with more recent volcanic activity and it breaks down quickly, releasing many different elements (potassium aluminum silicate, quartz, feldspar, and others) into the soil. These unique soils are much appreciated by winemakers and grape growers. Native Americans discovered the rock fractured in a curved or "conchoidal" fashion, which, carefully worked, produces excellently sharp cutting tools. Obsidian was traded very widely. The unique nature of each eruption has been key to understanding Native American movements over thousands of years. The exact shape of arrowheads is also important to dating. The Historic Courthouse Museum has a very interesting collection on display.

2 MILLION–10,000 YEAR OLD VOLCANICS

The young Clear Lake Volcanic Field consists of andesite, dacite, basalt, and rhyolite built up in complex sequence with volcanic ash and tuff thrown into the mix. Mt. Konocti propelled airborne volcanic matter over 5 ft. deep, past the cinder cones now to the east. The 4 main periods of volcanic activity have, however, mostly been non-explosive and have been punctuated with 200,000-year long "quiet" gaps. The most recent volcanic activity, creating cinder cones and maars, was 10,000 yrs. ago–so visiting in the next 190,000 yrs. is highly recommended.

Indigenous Inhabitants of Lake County

Native Americans have lived in Lake County for about 12,000 years and may well have witnessed the last major volcanic eruptions here 10,000 years ago. An abundance of water and a plentiful wild food supply attracted many different tribes here. Before European colonization it was thought to be one of the most dense concentrations of Native Americans in California. Hundreds of Pomo, Wappo, Lake Miwok, Wintun/Patwin and Yuki peoples all co-existed here, living in dozens of small independent tribal groups. Many different languages were used and at least 3 of the 7 distinctly different Pomo languages were likely spoken. Mostly hunter-gatherers rather than farmers, the tribal people moved about freely using well-established trails to Napa, the Pacific coast, and beyond for trade. Without metal, they fashioned tools from local obsidian rock (volcanic glass) to hunt elk, deer, and other wildlife. Lake and woodland vegetation supplied ample raw materials to construct fishing boats, multi-family dwellings, communal sweat lodges, and dance houses.

Top: A Pomo fishing boat constructed from tightly bound bundles of tule reeds.

Above: Tule reeds were also woven into wall and floor coverings, with white willow often used to make baby carriers.

Left: A tightly woven, waterproof, twined construction basket strong enough for cooking made from local willow and sedge root with redbud bark decoration.

Master Basketmakers

The Pomo had no pottery; instead they employed a great array of local plants to create baskets for all manner of purposes. Baskets were used for cooking, storage, transport, trapping, fishing, and many ceremonial purposes. Apart from the fishing baskets, it was mostly the women who produced these baskets. Baskets were not only functional, they were beautifully decorated. Over time the Pomo honed this art into what is now one of the most respected basket-making traditions in the world.

Left: 1900s photo of a large raised acorn storage basket/ granary from the Ukiah area. Acorns were a staple in the local Native Americans' diet. They were ground into a meal upon stone grinding bowls, then washed multiple times to leach out bitter flavors. Many storage baskets were hung off the ground to prevent spoilage.

Below: A coiled construction storage basket.

Above: A Pomo ceremonial basket adorned with bird feathers, quail plumes, and abalone decoration from the Historic Courthouse Museum collection.

Below: Polly Homes, a noted local artist, and her work.

WHERE TO SEE MORE

The Historic Courthouse Museum has an excellent collection of Pomo baskets, as well as many other interesting artifacts.

Historic Courthouse Museum
225 North Main Street, Lakeport, CA 95453
(707) 263-4555. Open Wed–Sat 10 am–4 pm,
Sunday noon–4 pm

Grace Hudson Museum
431 South Main Street, Ukiah, CA 95482
(707) 467-2836. Open Wed-Sat 10 am–4:30 pm
Sunday Noon–4:30 pm

Early Visitors, Pioneers, and Settlers

In the 1830s, other people began to discover the bounties of Lake County. Russian pelt and fur trapping teams arrived from the north, and a Spanish land grant given to Salvador Vallejo in 1844 brought herds of longhorn cattle from the south. In 1847 the first white settlers, Kelsey and Stone, arrived, brutally abused the Natives and paid the ultimate price. The 1849 Gold Rush and the establishment of California in 1850 brought a great wave of new settlers eager to stake a claim in the west. In 1854 the first of a succession of covered wagon trains arrived. Many crossed the plains from Missouri in arduous journeys in covered wagons; others arrived by steamship from the east coast. Some came to mine, but most of the permanent settlers were farmers who raised livestock, grain, and other vegetable crops.

Top left: *An early horse-powered hay baling machine in Lake County in the 1880s.*

Center left: *The Copsey family arrived in Lake County in 1855; one of the sons has extracted a cart of cinnabar from their Helen Mine near Middletown.*

Bottom left: *Teams of oxen haul logs at the Akers & Specks sawmill on Mt. Hannah.*

Top right: *Travelers to Lake County, c.1875, outside the Lake County House hotel and stage stop in Middletown. The horse-drawn stagecoach departed from Calistoga and took three hours to get over Mt. St. Helena on steep, winding dirt roads.*

Bottom right: *A natural artesian well gushes water from underground in the Scotts Valley area. Early homes near such powerful wells were able to pipe water to upstairs rooms.*

Early settlers soon began putting in fruit orchards and grapevines, recognizing the climate was ideally suited, having a cold dormant season and long hot summers. The settlements grew rapidly. In 1860 there were about 1,000 people registered; by 1870 about 2,500; and by 1880 over 6,000. Wood was needed to supply this rapid expansion and sawmills flourished in the Cobb, Elk, and Pine mountain areas. There were no redwoods, but local pines, firs, and cedar trees provided good lumber. Local geology brought the mining of cinnabar (a mixture of sulphur and quicksilver), the mercury extracted being essential in gold ore processing. It was water, however, from the same ground that really put Lake County on the map, as the discovery of many hot and cold mineral springs with "medicinal" effects drew visitors from all over the world.

WHERE TO SEE MORE

Lower Lake Schoolhouse Museum
A restored schoolhouse built in 1877 with many local settler artifacts.
16345 Main Street, Lower Lake
Tel. **(707) 995-3565**.
Open Wed–Sat 11 am-4 pm

The Ely Stage Stop
An original 1882 stage stop with old farming equipment and antique barns that house interesting events.
9921 Soda Bay Rd (1 mile from Highway 29 Junction), Kelseyville.
Tel: **(707) 533-9990**.
Open Sat-Sun 11 am-3 pm
Sunday noon—4.30pm

Tourism Erupts across Lake County

Lake County exploded as a tourist destination from the 1870s onward as word spread of its natural beauty and the beneficial effects of the waters. The large lake, encircled by mountains, reminded many immigrants of Europe. The reliable Mediterranean climate and pure air drew many from the San Francisco Bay Area to fish, sail, and hike in the wide open spaces. The unique local geology produced abundant natural springs that were hot, cold, and carbonated, with a wide array of differing mineral properties. World-class luxurious resorts, hotels, spas, and "sanitariums" appeared with remarkable speed all over the county, with claims to alleviate or cure a catalogue of medical ailments. "If you build it, they will come"–and they did, in the thousands.

Top left: An extravagantly themed Venetian Carnival held in Lakeport in 1897. The stage for Highlands Springs Resort, one of at least 18 resorts operating at the time, passes through a festival arch.

Center: Laurel Dell Resort on tranquil Blue Lakes was built by Henry Wambold in 1890. The dining room overlooked the lake and a small steamboat enabled guests to explore the lakes. He also owned the Blue Lake Bean Cannery in nearby Upper Lake.

Bottom left: Adams Springs Stage traveled from Calistoga three times a week. Guests from San Francisco came by ferry, then train, and finally this stage over Mt. St. Helena. This typical journey took over nine hours, and guests often stayed for months at a time to "take the waters."

Left: This large hotel complex, built in 1905, was an expansion of the original Witter Springs Hotel. It boasted 100 rooms. Sadly, the 1906 earthquake—and resultant decline in guests—halted its financial success. It closed in 1915, although the Witter Springs bottled water continued to be sold until the 1950s.

Below: A hiking party from Adams Springs Resort enjoys a healthy hike through mountain trails.

Opposite page, top right: The cozy open-sided oak cabin at Hobergs Resort was where guests could gather and sample the water.

Center left: A poster, circa 1885, advertising Highland Springs as "The Great Sanitarium of the West." It boasted the "only" golf links and "The best paid orchestra in the county" (how did the others sound?). Situated on 2,500 acres near Kelseyville, it also had croquet, tennis courts, riding stables, a bowling alley, and a dance hall. It could accommodate 400 guests (for $10 a week!) and had a dining room that could seat up to 500 people.

Left: Bathers enjoy soaking in the 86°F iron-rich pool at Newman Springs, built by a Swedish immigrant in 1898 in the hills near Bartlett and Upper Lake.

Before Wine...there was Water

Lake County was established officially in 1861. It was formed with the lake as its natural center by adjusting the boundaries of Napa, Mendocino, and Colusa counties. It had previously been known as the "Clear Lake Township of Napa County–Hot Springs Section." This was certainly a prophetic label as many thousands poured in from all over the world to take the waters for their health. One of the fastest growing resorts was Bartlett Springs, which turned from a few cabins in 1872 into a small town with its own shops, hotels, and cabins that could accommodate 5,000 people. The water's popularity led to a demand for it to be bottled and shipped. Bartlett Water traveled as far as Alaska, Honolulu, and Central America. Bartlett Springs Soda Water was also served on Cunard liners.

Top: The Bartlett Springs Mineral fountain with guests, circa 1890.

Left: Visitors to Bartlett, on the last leg of a very long four-part journey by ferry, train, stage, this boat from Lakeport, and then stage again.

Above: Contemporary advertisements. Allen Springs was close to Bartlett.

Right: Bartlett had a bowling alley and ballroom to amuse guests when not drinking or bathing.

Center: The bottling line crew. Bottling started in the 1880s. The first bottles had the Bartlett name molded into the glass, but later bottles such as these had labels attached. The water was naturally slightly carbonated so it needed a firm cap to seal it.

Bottom right: Local tules were ingeniously used to protect the bottles on their long and winding road to many far-flung markets.

Bottom left: Teams of eight white mules stand ready to haul a large volume of water over the hills.

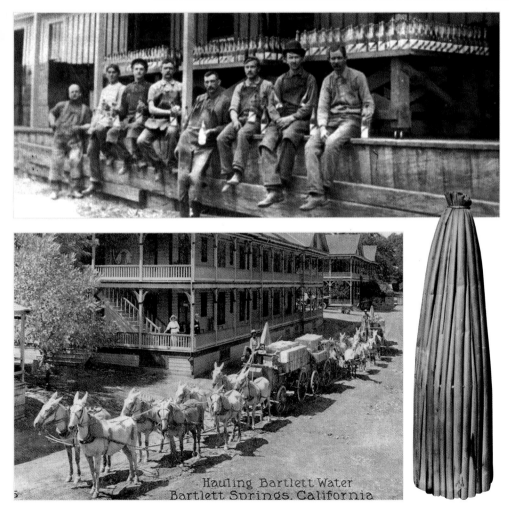

Hauling Bartlett Water
Bartlett Springs, California

The First Viticulturists

Vineyards quickly took root as the local soils and climate offered perfect growing conditions. From the mid-1850s early settlers planted small garden vineyards for their own use. Mission grapes from Spanish days were soon replaced with European varietals favored by the new immigrants. When miners, then tourists, began flocking into the county in the late 1870s, the wine industry was well underway. A lively mix of viticulturists had poured in. Some made wine to sell in bulk to the local market, others hauled grapes to the nearby towns of Calistoga and Ukiah. Lyons Creek vineyard (pictured below) was one of the first 50-acre vineyards with a winery to be put in near Scotts Valley around 1872.

Above: Serranus Clinton Hastings came to California in 1849 and struck gold in a meteoric legal career. Appointed California's First Chief Justice in 1851 and Attorney General in 1852, he then amassed a fortune in real estate, becoming one of California's largest landowners. He invested heavily in Napa and Lake counties and established 115 acres of vineyards across the county. He wrote botany books and had a plant genus, "Hastingsia," named after him, a lily that thrives on serpentine soils. In 1878 he founded Hastings College of the Law with a $100,000 gift. In 1885, as a widower of 70, he caused a social stir by marrying a 19-year-old Ukiah girl, Lillian Knust, and moving Lake County with her. A former lady friend then filed suit for breach of promise. He challenged her claims in the Superior Court of Lake County.

German neighbor Louis Berger planted a 36-acre vineyard and hauled wine over the Hopland grade, receiving 8 cents a gallon for his labors. Louis Kugelman moved to Lake County in 1877 for his health, settled near Lower Lake and set out 40 acres of vines. His thriving business sold wine for 10-15 cents a gallon, both in-and-out-of-county. He expanded and built a 20,000-gallon capacity winery. The California Agricultural Improvement Association, directed by R. K. Nichols, a local real estate agent, planted a 300-acre vineyard near Cache Creek. Previously called the Clear Lake Water Company, they built a dam across the creek (the only outlet of Clear Lake) which sparked a famous act of insurrection. In 1868, after successive heavy rains, the water level had risen to such an extent that many farmers were under water and disease was rampant, causing great distress. All legal appeals to get the level lowered failed. When the local judge incited the citizens to seek "a higher court," they took heed, and with elaborate military-style orchestration, 300 local men duly destroyed the dam!

Above: "Konockti," a 300-acre vineyard planted in Lower Lake by R. K. Nichols. From an 1884 contemporary lithograph.

Lake County's Wine Pioneers: 1859-1889

Winemaking began in the late 1850s and, like the county, grew rapidly. In 1882 there were over 600 acres under vine, and 1,754 by 1892 (5 times more than Mendocino). Some early winemakers supplied bulk wines to the local miners, while others had much grander ambitions and built large capacity stone wineries and vaults with a view to bottling and then exporting wine. Muscat, Riesling, Zinfandel, and Burgundy grape varieties were most planted. The "Golden Chasselas," often reported (below), was a popular varietal from Switzerland, Germany, and France–perhaps another reason why Lake County was then called " The Switzerland of America"!

Serranus C. Hastings (1881)
Bought a large ranch in Upper Lake and arranged for a 115-acre vineyard of Zinfandel, Franken Riesling, and Muscat grapes to be planted. By 1886 he had a 150,000-gallon winery & distillery. In 1889 he reported 120 tons of Zinfandel grapes.

Charles Hammond (1885)
Harvard graduate, studied at the famous Inglenook Winery. Bought 600 acres and put in a 30-acre vineyard. Reported 50 tons of Zinfandel in 1889. Known to have also planted Cabernet Sauvignon and Sémillion. In 1893 he exhibited wine at the World's Fair in Chicago.

Louis P. Berger (1879)
Planted a 35-acre vineyard of mixed varieties. He hauled wine over the Hopland grade.

Lyons Creek Vyd. (1872)
John Lyons, a winemaker, built a winery and planted 50 acres of mixed varieties.

T. H. Buckingham (1875)
Wealthy S.F. shoe magnate. Planted a 70-acre vineyard including "Zinfandel, Muscatel, Burger, Golden Chasselas; also some Sauvignon Vert, Le Noir, Emperor, and Flaming Tokay," noted varieties in 1882.

Louis Kugelman (1877)
Moved up from Napa to improve his asthma. He planted 40 acres of vineyards: Zinfandel, Burger, and Golden Chasselas grapes. In 1890 he built a 20,000-gallon capacity winery. The wine was sold locally and also transported in bulk in 100-gallon puncheons to nearby quicksilver mines.

George Wrey (1883)
Wealthy British industrialist. Bought 5,000 acres south of Lower Lake, employed fellow Brit Maurice Keatinge to plant a 100-acre vineyard of Golden Chasselas, Gutedel, Riesling, and Zinfandel. Nicolai built him a 20,000-gallon capacity winery. In 1891 Keatinge reported 40,000 gallons of wine being produced from the 100 acres.

David Lobree (1882)
Planted a 35-acre vineyard of Burgundy and Chasselas grapes on Dead Horse Flat in Middletown.

W. C. Mottier (1875)
A noted local winemaker near Harbin in Middletown, dubbed "professor" due to successful experiments with native Californian vines.

Ralph K. Nichols (1882)
Took over the ill-fated Clear Lake Water Company site, near Cache Creek. Poetically re-named as the "The California Agriculture and Improvement Association," a 300-acre vineyard of Burger, Zinfandel, and Chasselas grapes was planted on site from 1882-84. In 1889 they built a wooden winery and blasted enormous wine vaults into the rocky hill-sides. The large tunnels were designed to hold 500,000 gallons of wine! The tunnels sadly collapsed. In 1889 they harvested 600 tons of grapes.

Stephen Nicolai (1884)
A Prussian master stone-mason (who built the Wrey winery and Lower Lake jail). Planted 10 acres west of Voight and built a stone winery for himself.

Tobias Bilsbach (1884)
Fellow Prussian planted a vineyard next to Nicolai and hired him to build a winery. 8 acres of Zinfandel and Chasselas recorded to T. "Billesback" in 1889.

David Voight (1872)
One of the earliest wine-makers. Respected grower who planted a 16-acre vineyard on Morgan Valley Road, near Copsey Creek. Claimed 6 tons of fruit per acre. Planted Zinfandel and Riesling.

Thomas Allen (1859)
The first official record of winemaking in the county. U.S. Agriculture Census in 1860 noted he had 1,200 gallons of wine in storage.

Lillie Langtry (1888)
Famous English actress who bought a 4,190-acre ranch in Guenoc Valley. She hired Henri Descelles, a wine-maker from Bordeaux, to take charge of the 20-acre vineyard and winery already on the property. In 1890 50 tons of Burgundy grapes were harvested. She declared the resulting Claret, with her face upon the label, to be the "finest in America."

The Wine Industry Flourishes

In 1883, wealthy Englishman George Wrey bought 5,000 acres just south of Lower Lake. Wrey had coal mines in Scotland, orange groves in Florida, and a sheep ranch in Australia. Attracted by the area's success with fruit growing, he employed winemaker Maurice Keatinge to plant orchards and a 100-acre vineyard. He planted Zinfandel, Gutedel, Golden Chasselas, and Riesling varietals, amongst others. Wrey also got local stonemason Stephen Nicolai to build a 20,000-gallon capacity winery (shown above). The impressive winery was cleverly located on the hillside so that the wine could be moved by gravity, the crush facilities being on the top and the fermenting being on the floor below. Wrey had further plans to excavate tunnels for storage and install a bottling plant. A severe drought in Australia and bad frosts in Florida halted these grander plans. The winery supplied bulk wine to Greystone Winery in St. Helena for many years before his son closed it during Prohibition in the 1920s.

Left: Stephen Nicolai also built this stone jail in Lower Lake. It is still the smallest jail in the country that remains standing. The story is that the builders purposely got themselves arrested for drunkenness the night it was completed so as to go down in history as its first occupants. They escaped through the roof—of course they knew exactly how to.

THE FIRST WINE BOOM

The young Lake County wine industry reached its peak in 1892. In that year there were 1,794 acres of vineyards, 48 winegrape growers and 8 wineries officially recorded in the county.

What were they drinking then?

Zinfandel, a full-bodied, deep red grape (from Croatia) had become the most popular winegrape in California by the end of the 19th century. Lake County viticulturists readily embraced it, too. In 1891 Zinfandel was easily the most popular variety on record. Another local favorite was "Golden Chasselas" (of Swiss origin). The white wines they would have enjoyed were likely of a Swiss/German, light/fruity wine style. Charles Wetmore, the "Commissioner at Large" for the State Viticultural Commission, when visiting the county in 1880 declared, "Lake County is certainly destined to become famed for its Clarets and light white wines. It is, I believe, the true 'Rhine' district of California." He gives us an interesting contemporary perspective. Sweet dessert wines were also very popular in the late nineteenth century, which accounts for the large amounts of Muscat and Tokay planted by these early winemakers.

Lillie Langtry was a sparkling addition to Lake County's wine scene (page 78). Guenoc had been purchased by her, sight unseen. It was found for her by General Barnes, an attorney who had also previously secured American citizenship for her in 1887. Upon her first visit, in 1888, she gratefully asked Barnes to "Join me in Paradise." She came with quite the entourage: a French gardener and a British Butler, "Beverley," who by all accounts attracted more local fascination than she did, becoming popular for his tall tales of high society. She was delighted to find existing vineyards and a stone winery, built 10 years earlier by previous owner Thomas Musick. Of course, she needed a French winemaker, so Henri Descelles, a "capable man from Bordeaux," was hired to make wine. In 1889 she produced 50 tons of "Burgundy" grapes from 20 acres of vines. Not one to miss a marketing opportunity (having already loaned her face to sell soaps and cigarettes), a wine label with her portrait upon it was designed. She declared it "the best Claret in America." Lillie and romantic beau Fred Gebhard had big plans to breed race horses on their adjoining properties, but those plans sadly fell apart–as did their relationship. In 1906 she sold Guenoc, 12 days before the San Francisco earthquake.

Interestingly, this portrait entitled "The Dean's Daughter" was the one chosen for the wine label. More a nod to her demure roots as the daughter of a Jersey pastor than her later life as consort of royalty and international stage star. In 1897 a Lake County Judge finally granted her the divorce she had sought for years from Edward Langtry, her peskily tenacious British husband.

Above: Anton Wagner bought this stone winery and ten-acre vineyard in 1910 from Tobias Bilsbach and continued to make wine right up to (and beyond!) Prohibition. Right: T.H. Buckingham made a fortune with the Buckingham and Hecht shoe factory in San Francisco. In 1875 he purchased 1,100 acres of land near Kelseyville on a peninsula 2 miles long that juts out into the lake. "Buckingham Park," as it was called, had a powerful steam pump that hauled water out of the lake to gravity feed the house and lush gardens. It also irrigated 70 acres of vineyards. In 1884 Zinfandel, Golden Chasselas, Muscatel, Burger, Sauvignon Vert, Le Noir, Flaming Tokay, and Emperor grapes grew. In 1891 George A. Buckingham reported 75 tons of Zinfandel and Muscat.

"Pure" Politics, and the Wine Industry Stalls

Pictured above is the Main Street in Upper Lake in the early 1880s. Quite remarkably, it still looks like this, a typical example of main streets right across the county then. Imagine: you get off the stage (or park your horse), you stroll into the Blue Wing Saloon for a pick-me-up (it's been a long ride), you then happily retire, right next door, to the comforts of the Tallman Inn. Sound good? Apparently not to the Anti-Saloon League or the Women's Christian Temperance Union (W.C.T.U.), who decided it just would not do at all. So with Bible in one hand and ax in the other, they set about changing things. The "Progressive Era" of U.S. politics had begun! What an amazing cultural and political melting pot the whole fifty year period between 1870-1920 must have been, particularly out in California's "wild west," where they were all just getting acquainted. Lake County had its own political squabbles: where the county seat should be, for example, which took no fewer than 3 votes, plus a recount, to decide. In 1870, Lakeport (not Lower Lake) was chosen. In 1867, in the midst of all this, the Courthouse mysteriously burnt down. The new "pure" political activists cited that there were more saloons than churches or schools in main streets across America, and believed these were destroying family life.

Above: Carrie Nation, an early W.C.T.U. warrior, was frequently refused service on her forays into U.S. saloons. Maybe the ax was off-putting! She started two campaign magazines: "Smashers Mail" and "The Hatchet."

Below: Choose your paperwork. Some signed the pledge. Post-Prohibition some got their doctors to sign something.

Below left: As is often the case, God was claimed to be on everyone's side.

Above: In 1888 Kelseyville briefly incorporated to buy out the only saloon in town and become "dry." In 1909 (pictured above) they were a little more evenly divided wet/dry! Local Option Elections were held each year until 1918.

Above: Family and patriotism were mobilized as reasons to vote "Dry." The two checked issues relate to Prohibition. The third relates to Women's Suffrage, which was very entwined with the Temperance movement in the 1880s. California women got the vote in 1911. A narrow Suffragist win was achieved by targeting rural areas, as city-based saloon and business interest groups feared a vote for women would be a Prohibition vote.

Right: Anna Morrison Reed, poet, activist, circa 1913. On an anti-Prohibition lecture tour with the Grape Growers Association.

Campaigning became intense from the late 19th Century onwards. Many prominent speakers came to Lake County, which by then had four very active Women's Temperance "Unions." At first individual counties could decide for themselves whether to be "Wet" and allow liquor licenses or "Dry" and not. In 1874 the County held a "Local Option Election" on the issue. In Kelseyville and Middletown the vote was close. The townsfolk of Kelseyville had a habit of buying up saloons to close them–so not surprising. Lower Lake, however, was tied, which was surprising as the wine industry was really taking off near there. In the run up to Prohibition there were ever more propositions on the ballot. The Prop 2 referred to on the car (shown below) is from the 1914 or 1916 state elections. Vineyard owners went from concerned to devastated when in 1919 the 18th Amendment prohibiting the manufacture of alcohol was adopted, the only one to have a delayed start date. Prohibition officially began in 1920 and lasted until its repeal in 1933. The Lake County wine industry was forced to go dormant.

Lake County Turns to Other Fruit (and Nuts)

The wine industry now nipped in the bud, Lake County revisited fruits that were popular in the pioneer days. Apples, pears, all kinds of stone fruits, almonds, and walnuts had all grown very well back then. In 1885 California exhibited fruit from across the state at The World's Fair in New Orleans. Lake County attracted world-wide attention with a 2 lb. apple and a Bartlett pear weighing over 1 lb. The soon-to-be internationally famous pear industry had begun. In 1885 Thomas Porteus planted four acres of Bartletts in Big Valley. In the Scotts Valley and Kelseyville areas others also planted pear orchards. The biggest challenge for early pear growers was how to get pears to market with mountain roads and no railway (often promised but never seen). In 1887 J. B. Laughlin and L. P. Clendenin built the first pear drying yard. Other early pioneer families, such as the Annettes and the Hendersons, with hundreds of acres followed suit. By 1922 Lake County was the dried pear capital of the world.

Above left: The County exhibit at the California State Fair (circa 1920). Prominently displayed are two boxes of large pears (probably Bartletts). The man with the bow tie is touching a collection of Lake County walnuts. The bottles behind him are not wine (obviously), but bottled Bartlett water. The man far right has behind him a fine display of Native American Pomo baskets made in Lake County.

Above right: The 1926 California State Fair Exhibition now has the Lake County pear firmly on its pedestal as the County's prized crop. Spectacular contemporary advertising art is on the boxes.

Above: Red walnuts from Alex M. Suchan, a very well-respected local walnut nurseryman. He started in the mid-1950s and has supplied trees and educated many new walnut farmers.

Left: Walnuts are harvested by shaking the trees and bagging up the nuts. Note the vineyards in the background—a typical county scen

Top Left: In 1888 Frank W. Gibson bought 440 acres of land half a mile southwest of Lakeport and started the 120-acre "Glenwood Ranch." He planted 15 acres of fruit, mostly prunes and also some figs. His fruit is pictured drying in the sun. He also built the "Lakeport Canning Company" on site and was an early pioneer in canning fruit. Canned figs were his speciality.

Left: Pears drying in wooden boxes in the Finley area, circa 1918.

Below: A natural "Integrated Pest Management" system in action at Diane Henderson's pioneer-planted pear farm in Kelseyville. The cabinet puffs female codling moth pheromones out across the orchards, which confuse the male moths rendering them unable to find a mate, and create worm damage in the pears. Lewis Henderson planted the first 20 acres of pears here in 1891.

Pears were halved, cored, and then dried for several days in the Lake County sunshine. Nearly all local pears were processed this way until 1923. Europe had been the main market for these dried pears, but suddenly that market fell away due to European troubles. Pear growers turned to growing fruit for both the fresh and domestic canned pear markets. Fresh shipments were initially sent to local and western markets and later the advent of refrigerated cars permitted shipments to eastern markets from railheads in Mendocino County. In the 1940s and 1950s Lake County had more than 10 packing houses, and pears were also sent to more than 20 California canners for processing. Today, while the industry is smaller in acreage, Lake County continues to be recognized as the premium California district for fresh pears. In 1909 John B. Hendricks, with the help of Oscar Poe, began a 50-acre walnut orchard of "Frankettes" and "Poes" in Scotts Valley, the largest in the county then. These men, along with Roy Summers and Walter Reichert, helped expand the walnut acreage county-wide and they grafted most of the large walnut trees still seen across the county. Post-Prohibition, the County's vineyards were largely taken out and replaced by pears and walnuts. It is ironic that today the exact reverse is true.

Above: Scully Packing Company's Finley shed is on the site of the first pear packing facility in the county built in the 1920s by Lowell Annette. 3 sheds in the county sort pears for size and grade today. About half the crop is sent to canners, driers, and juicers. The rest is packaged for the fresh market. Lake County produces 40% of all California's fresh pear shipments because the Lake County pear is known for its exceptional flavor, shelf life, and attractive shape. About 20% of the fresh crop is exported, and the rest is enjoyed domestically from coast to coast.

The 1960s and the Wine Industry Swings Back

It wasn't until the mid 1960s that California began to take off as a wine region. Robert Mondavi built his Napa winery in 1965. The famous Stephen Spurrier (some say *spur-i-ous*) "judgment of Paris" blind taste-off, which pronounced California wines more "*form-i-dable*" than French ones, happened in 1976. That publicity helped put California (back) on the map of world-class wine producers. Given this backdrop, one must admire the vision and pluck of the early Lake County growers who put in vineyards in the mid-1960s. When Walt and Madelene Lyon moved home to the Big Valley ranch where Madelene was born, a friend suggested the land might be perfect for winegrapes. In 1966 they decided to try it. Their first Cabernet Sauvignon cuttings were given to them by Nathan Fay, who owned vineyards right next to Stag's Leap (the Lyons made their own cuttings). A little later Walt and fellow local grower Reid Dorn needed to sell their grapes. They heard Napa wineries were short of grapes, so they headed out to the Napa Valley together. The first place they tried was Robert Mondavi, who snapped up their grapes, with a handshake, on the spot! The supply of Lake's grapes to Napa had begun. The other early winegrape adventurer was Myron Holdenried. He had inherited good pioneering genes; his ancestors were amongst the earliest European settlers in 1856. His great-grandfather, Lewis Henderson, was one of the first pear farmers in the county. Myron also started his vineyards in 1966, planting 30 acres of Zinfandel on a former cattle pasture. He and his wife Marilyn grew that to 150 acres of many different varietals. They started the successful Wildhurst winery, in 1991. By 1970 the acreage of Lake County vineyards was up to 520 acres–and winegrapes were back. The Lower Lake Winery, built in 1977 by the Stuermer family, was the county's first post-Prohibition winery. They produced Cabernet and White Cabernet from local grapes.

Top left: Madelene and Walt Lyon were one of the very first farmers to start replanting winegrapes post Prohibi tion in Lake County. They are shown here mid-harvest in October 1973, (wi Mount Konocti behind them). They are loading their Cabernet Sauvignon grap from Big Valley into an old pear bin wh they have lined ready to haul the grap over to the Napa Valley

Top right: Marilyn and Myron Holdenrie also planted some of the very first vineyards in Lake County back in 1966 They also converted the historic Odd Fellows building in downtown Kelseyville into a lovely tasting room for their wine

Below: Ron Bartolucci and his daughter Deanna represent a third and fourth generation of winegrape growers. Ron's grandfather immigrated from Italy in 1913, bringing a love of winemaking and grape growing with him. Both Ron and Deanna organically farm their vineyards in Lake County.

In 1979 a 26-member growers' association called Lake County Cellars built Konocti Winery in Kelseyville. The group hired André Tchelistcheff to consult and made some very well-received wines before disbanding. In 1963 the Magoon family acquired Guenoc Ranch, with a passion to realize Lillie Langtry's 1890s dream of producing world-class wine from the property. In the early 1970s they planted a dozen classic French varietals and, in 1982, built a beautiful 100,000-case winery. In 1979 Jess Jackson converted an 80-acre pear and walnut orchard in Lakeport into vineyards. For several years he sold his grapes to wineries such as Fetzer. When a shift in the market in 1981 left Jackson's grapes unsold, he did the "only thing we could do–make wine." In 1982 Kendall-Jackson released their first "Chateau du Lac" label. Jackson recruited Jed Steele to be his winemaker. Jed's passion for winemaking was a key part of their phenomenal growth. Jed left that empire at the "million cases a year mark" to start up his own highly successful label, Steele Wines, and later the aptly named Shooting Star.

Top: The wonderful mural on the side of Jed Steele's winery in Kelseyville was painted by a talented group of students from the local Kelseyville High School. The 70,000-case capacity winery sits on the site of the original Mt. Konocti Winery that the original Lake County cooperative built in 1979. Jed Steele and his son Quincy (who has his own "Writers Block" wine label) make an incredible collection of wines, many from more unusual grape varietals. Over half of the grapes they source are locally grown. Jed is a winemaker's winemaker with incredible depth and breadth of knowledge, who likes to experiment. He has taught other winemakers in the county, who now make their own wine.

The Fetzer Vineyards, based in Mendocino County, were the first to place a Lake County appellation on bottles in the early 1970s. In 1982 they made 95,000 cases of wine from Lake grapes and 90% of it carried the appellation. Cabernet Sauvignon, Zinfandel, Muscat Canelli, Riesling, and Sauvignon Blanc were the main varietals they purchased. Ron Bartolucci was director of vineyard operations for Fetzer, (and helped them start organic farming), so he knew Lake County well before starting his own vineyards here in 1973. He now has four ranches, and both Ron and his daughter Deanna organically farm their vineyards. In 1984 there were 3,000 acres of vineyards in the county; today there are over 9,400. The number of new wineries has increased 12-fold; there are currently over 40 and increasing. Lake County is deciding to hang onto its prized fruit–to create its own exceptional quality wines. These owners' and winemakers' stories are told here.

Viticulture & Winemaking in Lake County

From Farming to Land Stewardship

Left: Sheep roam freely through the fall vineyards and ancient oaks on the Six Sigma Ranch and Winery. Kaj and Else Ahlmann have placed a conservation easement on their 4,300-acre property to preserve the beautiful, pristine land and its many natural inhabitants for future generations. They raise sheep, cattle and pigs and their organically raised meat is in great demand locally.

Below: A ladybug getting to work on the Six Sigma ranch. They release many thousands of these beneficial insects into the vineyards each year if they need to. Custom predator "cuvées" help to crush unwanted pests and mites, employing Mother Nature rather than chemical sprays.

Lake County has the cleanest air and some of the largest tracts of public lands in California. The county's wide open spaces and rich agricultural heritage have produced spectacular scenery. Grape growers, passionate to protect this pristine landscape for future generations, have embraced sustainable farming. Over 70% of wine-growers in the region have participated in the award-winning Code of Sustainable Winegrowing Program, devised by the non-profit CSWA (California Sustainable Winegrowing Alliance). The program promotes the latest, environmentally-sound farming practices that help manage and conserve natural resources, build healthy ecosystems, and also develop social and economic sustainability. Ron Bartolucci has been organically farming winegrapes in the county since 1973. There are now over 20 other growers registered as organic. A few are biodynamically certified. A strong belief in land stewardship and preservation has seen some ecologically-minded owners place conservation easements on their lands, or establish large wildlife preserves on them, protecting these incredible habitats.

Above: A mustard cover crop between the vines at Brassfield Estate Winery in the spring. Cover crops are a natural way to add nitrogen to soil, prevent soil erosion and limit dust. Jerry Brassfield, the owner, has set aside 1,000 acres of this idyllic property as a wildlife preserve.

Left: Native Tule Elk greeted Bill "Poppo" Van Pelt on his first visit to the future Cache Creek Winery site. Deeply moved, he dedicated 520 of its 590 acres to elk and other wildlife an impressive legacy blending world-class grapes and conservation.

SUSTAINABLE

Virtually all of Lake's grape growers are using sustainable farming methods. The many "Soft, Safe, Sound" practices illustrated on these pages are not only focused on preserving the natural environment for future generations, but are also seeking to promote social and economic health in the community.

ORGANIC

Organic wines made from organically grown grapes are farmed without the use of any non-organic substances such as synthetic fertilizers, pesticides, fungicides, or herbicides. Wines that are labeled organic cannot have any added sulfites. Some sulfites occur naturally, but no more than 20 parts per million is permissible.

BIODYNAMIC

Some wineries in Lake County are biodynamically farmed. This method was devised in the 1920s by Rudolf Steiner, an Austrian scientist and philosopher who advocated holistic farming practices. His vision was to create a unified, more self-contained ecosystem that respects the many "life forces" involved in farming. These involve celestial influences, and timing of practices in tune with lunar cycles is key. Great emphasis is also placed on biodiversity, employing animals and composting to create healthy soils. Among the more esoteric aspects is the number of complex "preparations" required to be created and applied. One important ingredient used is silica, which interestingly often occurs naturally in many Lake County soils.

LAKE COUNTY'S NATURAL ADVANTAGE

The region has a head start when it comes to environmentally friendly farming practices. Crystal clear air, hot summers, stronger UV light, and dry air (fog is uncommon here) are all perfect conditions for winegrape growing. The county's main vineyards are between 1,360 and 3,000 feet above sea level, much higher than adjoining wine regions. The high elevation produces much colder winters and big diurnal temperature changes in the summer (which can turn 90°F days into 50°F nights). The county's isolation as a result of the Mayacamas and Vaca Ranges gives substantial protection from exotic vineyard pests such as the glassy-winged sharpshooter and European grapevine moth, reducing the need to spray for them. The county's agriculture department has a rigorous trapping and inspection program to monitor pests. They promote "Soft, Safe, and Sound" integrated pest management practices, which are widely adopted. Beneficial insects, cover crops, organic composts, controlling canopy air flow, and balancing vine vigor are all natural methods employed to create healthy vines that are more able to resist disease.

Above: Snow can be seen on the top of Snow Mountain from the Beckstoffer Vineyards in Amber Knolls Vineyard. Cold winters and cool summer nights help keep a wide variety of pests from establishing themselves here, reducing the need for many (or any) pesticide sprays.

Right: Gregory Graham wanted his winery in the Red Hills to be as environmentally friendly as possible, so he designed the winery roof to hold a large array of solar panels. They capture enough sunlight to power the whole facility. Happily, the winery gives him a zero electricity bill, and in his (non-existent) spare time he likes to watch his electricity meter run backwards.

The New Viticulturists

Lake County's winegrapes have been appreciated by the wine cognoscenti for years. The list of famous labels and winemakers who've used Lake's grapes (in a supporting role) reads like the winemaking Oscars. Today things are very different; the days of being a secret "diamond in the rough" are gone, but the diamonds are still here, right where they have always been, in the soil. Prominent grapegrower Andy Beckstoffer, who was key to raising the quality of Napa's grapes, is a strong advocate for the region. He has invested in over 1,000 acres of vineyards in the Red Hills, mostly planted to Cabernet Sauvignon. Reynaldo Robledo, famous Sonoma winemaker, owns 85 acres and says he can grow "everything" in Lake County. He likes the tropical notes he obtains from his Sauvignon Blanc vineyards in Big Valley.

Above: One of the Beckstoffer Cabernet vineyar in the Red Hills AVA. They convert sound viticult knowledge, the latest technology, and sustainabl farming methods into ultra-premium grapes.

Top: A newly planted vineyard in the Red Hills AVA area. The bright red, mineral-rich volcanic soils and sloping hillsides are typical of the region. This undulating landscape offers a wide variety of terroirs and microclimates. Wines are emerging from this AVA that are not only designated as coming from a single vineyard, but also some small-lot wines are produced from particular blocks, or "sweet spots," within those vineyards.

Left: Reynaldo Robledo is an award-winning winemaker from Sonoma who has had several of his wines poured at the White House. He was particularly excited by flavors found in his Sauvignon Blanc grapes from the vineyards he planted in the Big Valley AVA.

Right: Paul Zellman, a local viticulturist and consultant (far left), and Randy Krag, viticulturist for Beckstoffer Vineyards (far right), both helped develop and now teach the Master Vigneron Academy^{sm} *program each year, put on by the Lake County Winegrape Commission. A class of Master Vigneron graduates celebrate their recent graduation in front of Mt. Konocti.*

Below: A vineyard worker pruning vines in the spring on the Noggle vineyards.

WHO'S CRUSHING LAKE'S GRAPES?

The list of prestigious name winemakers and wine brands who are admirers of Lake County winegrapes is very long. In some cases these relationships go back over 30 years, such as that with Kendall-Jackson, who started out in Lake County.

Arnot-Roberts

Bodkin Wines

Bogle

Bonterra Vineyards

Cameron Hughes

Cinnabar

DeLoach

Hagafen

Jacuzzi Family

Joel Gott

Line 39

Michael David

Naked Wines

Oro en Paz

Peter Franus

Pine Ridge

Rock Wall

sidebar

Van Ruiten

THE LAKE COUNTY MASTER VIGNERON ACADEMY^{SM}

This ground-breaking program of structured learning in best vineyard practices was developed by the Lake County Winegrape Commission. It is the first of its kind and is taught in Spanish, adding the important human dimension to sustainability objectives. Recognizing the vital role vineyard supervisors play in producing world-class winegrapes gave Randy Krag the idea for a course. Paul Zellman, fellow viticulturist, stepped in to help develop and teach it. Students are selected from vineyards across the county for their passion, experience, and dedication to viticulture. They attend a year-long training (one day a month) visiting vineyards, wineries, UC Davis, and trade shows. Sessions target specific topics such as vineyard propagation or vineyard economics. The Credential of Master Vigneron^{cm} is a highly-regarded qualification by graduates and the wine industry. Establishing a highly-trained and well-appreciated workforce is seen as key to creating a bright, long-term future for this dynamic wine region.

Lake County Soils

The amazingly rich geology of this region has produced some unique soils, each proving to be increasingly sought -after terroir for the 9,400+ acres currently planted to vineyards. The viticultural soil types fall into four broad categories: mountain and hillside soils formed on a variety of volcanic materials; hillside soils formed on uplifted Franciscan and Great Valley Formations; upland alluvial soils on terraces; and lowland alluvial soils found in valleys. Each offers many exciting possibilities to viticulturists.

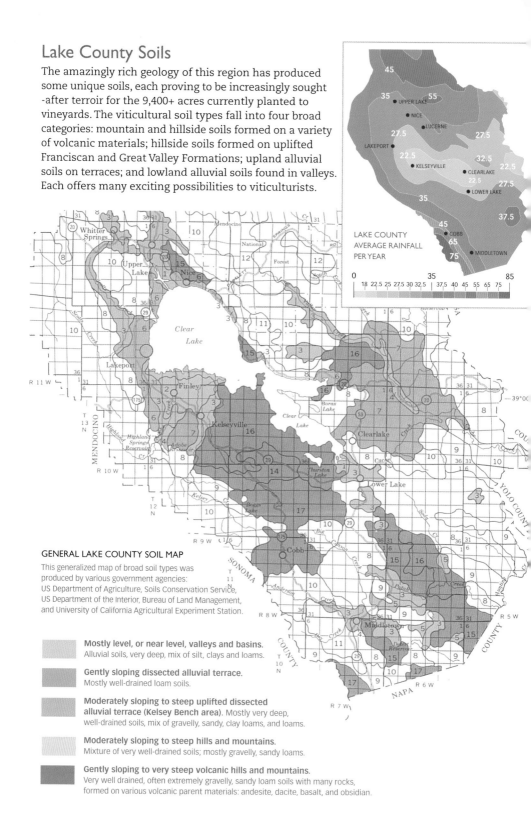

LAKE COUNTY
AVERAGE RAINFALL
PER YEAR

0   35   85

18 22.5 25 27.5 30 32.5 | 37.5 40 45 55 65 75

GENERAL LAKE COUNTY SOIL MAP

This generalized map of broad soil types was produced by various government agencies:
US Department of Agriculture, Soils Conservation Service,
US Department of the Interior, Bureau of Land Management,
and University of California Agricultural Experiment Station.

Mostly level, or near level, valleys and basins.
Alluvial soils, very deep, mix of silt, clays and loams.

Gently sloping dissected alluvial terrace.
Mostly well-drained loam soils.

Moderately sloping to steep uplifted dissected alluvial terrace (Kelsey Bench area). Mostly very deep, well-drained soils, mix of gravelly, sandy, clay loams, and loams.

Moderately sloping to steep hills and mountains.
Mixture of very well-drained soils; mostly gravelly, sandy loams.

Gently sloping to very steep volcanic hills and mountains.
Very well drained, often extremely gravelly, sandy loam soils with many rocks, formed on various volcanic parent materials: andesite, dacite, basalt, and obsidian.

Established 1991
BENMORE VALLEY AVA*

TOTAL IN AVA: 1,440 acres
VINEYARDS: N/A
ELEVATION: 2,400-2,700 feet
DEGREE-DAY Region I
RAINFALL: 40-50+ inches
SOILS: Alluvial (Manzanita loam)

Largely historic appellation named after a famous cattle rustler. At time of establishment planted with 125 acres of Chardonnay grapes. Recorded Region I rating may be questionable.

Lake County AVAs

Lake County sits within California's North Coast AVA (along with Napa, Sonoma, and Mendocino). The county has a further seven sub-appellations, however, that are exclusive to it. Climate, topography, and soils are some of the many factors used to determine an AVA. All of Lake's sub-appellations are united by high elevation, lack of fog, and the moderating effect of the lake on local climate. More than 85% of grapes must be from the stated appellation to use that name on the wine bottle.

Established 1983
NORTH COAST AVA

TOTAL IN AVA:
3,000,000 acres

Established 1984
CLEAR LAKE AVA*

TOTAL IN AVA: 168,960 acres
VINEYARDS: 500 acres
ELEVATION: 1,300-1,800 feet
DEGREE-DAY: Regions II-III
RAINFALL: 15-40 inches
SOILS: Franciscan, Volcanic, Alluvial

Originally established to encompass the traditional fertile farming valleys of Scotts Valley, Upper Lake, Big Valley, Lower Lake and Clearlake Oaks.

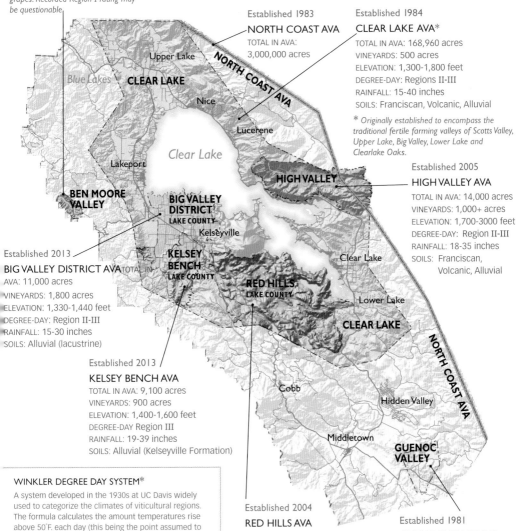

Established 2005
HIGH VALLEY AVA

TOTAL IN AVA: 14,000 acres
VINEYARDS: 1,000+ acres
ELEVATION: 1,700-3000 feet
DEGREE-DAY: Region II-III
RAINFALL: 18-35 inches
SOILS: Franciscan, Volcanic, Alluvial

Established 2013
BIG VALLEY DISTRICT AVA

TOTAL IN AVA: 11,000 acres
VINEYARDS: 1,800 acres
ELEVATION: 1,330-1,440 feet
DEGREE-DAY: Region II-III
RAINFALL: 15-30 inches
SOILS: Alluvial (lacustrine)

Established 2013
KELSEY BENCH AVA

TOTAL IN AVA: 9,100 acres
VINEYARDS: 900 acres
ELEVATION: 1,400-1,600 feet
DEGREE-DAY Region III
RAINFALL: 19-39 inches
SOILS: Alluvial (Kelseyville Formation)

Established 2004
RED HILLS AVA

TOTAL IN AVA: 31,397 acres
VINEYARDS: 4,000 acres
ELEVATION: 1,350-3000+ feet*
DEGREE-DAY Region III-IV
RAINFALL: 24-45 inches
SOILS: Volcanic (various)
*Most vineyards over 2,000 ft

Established 1981
GUENOC VALLEY AVA

TOTAL IN AVA: 4,396 acres
VINEYARDS: 400 acres
ELEVATION: 800-1,800 feet
DEGREE-DAY Region III-IV
RAINFALL: 45-55 inches
SOILS: Volcanic and Alluvial

WINKLER DEGREE DAY SYSTEM*

A system developed in the 1930s at UC Davis widely used to categorize the climates of viticultural regions. The formula calculates the amount temperatures rise above 50°F. each day (this being the point assumed to trigger vine growth). These numbers are then tallied over a fixed growing season (April-October) to establish a Region on a Scale of I-V.

Region I – the coolest (similar to Champagne or Rhine)
Region I I – (similar to the Bordeaux area of France)
Region I I I – (similar to the Rhône area of France)
Region I V – (similar to southern Spain and Portugal)
Region V – the hottest (not found in Lake County)

Individual sites can vary greatly from the generalizations shown

Guenoc Valley AVA (1981)

Located just a couple of miles from the Napa County line in southeastern Lake County, the Guenoc Valley AVA was not only the first AVA to be established in the county but was also the first single-proprietor AVA granted in America. Orville Magoon, the pioneering owner, was convinced that "Lake County will produce the great wines of the world" and to prove it proceeded to build the beautiful 54,000 square ft. winery that still operates today. The Guenoc Valley had attracted earlier winemakers. Early settlers planted winegrapes in that area and had even built a winery by the time Lillie Langtry acquired it in 1888. Today that fine winemaking vision and tradition still flourishes.

VINEYARD ELEVATION

Range: 800–1,800 feet.

WINES

A vast array of different soils and microclimates makes for a very fine tasting visit. The varietals are carefully matched and managed in their different terroirs. Sauvignon Blanc and Chardonnay, with tropical fruit from the valley floors, Cabernet Sauvignon from high on the volcanic hillsides, and the Petite Sirah from the valley magma are all great wines.

THE TERROIR/MESOCLIMATE

This appellation was a part of "Rancho Guenoc," a Mexican land grant dating back to 1854. The high elevation of the vineyards and large diurnal temperature swings, from 100˚F+ summer daytime temperatures that can drop to 50˚ F at night, provide beneficial cooling to the vines. The AVA's volcanic past is evident in the steep rocky ridges which have thin tufa or compacted ash soils, similar to those found in the very best Bordeaux sites, and have been planted with the same varietals. The valley floor has a great variety of soils, including well-drained shallow Cole clay loams and Still stratified alluvium soils (left). Pockets of solidified magma, high in magnesium, have been planted with Petite Sirah. Guenoc has the oldest known grapevine in the county, planted in 1850.

STILL LOAM /STRATIFIED SOIL

VARIETALS GROWN

SAUVIGNON BLANC • CHARDONNAY
CABERNET SAUVIGNON • VIOGNIER
PETITE SIRAH • CABERNET FRANC
PETIT VERDOT • MARSANNE

LAKE WINERIES

Langtry Estate & Vineyards

Clear Lake AVA (1984)

Jess Jackson, of Kendall-Jackson fame, started his first winery in Lake County, converting a pear and walnut orchard into his "Chateau du Lac" winery. A familiar story now, but in 1982 when he applied for appellation status for the area there were just 3 wineries and 3,000 acres under vine. The successful application recognized a number of important factors: the lake moderates the climate of the adjacent lands, warming them in winter and cooling them in summer; there is a lack of marine fog and winds prevalent in other wine regions; and there are dramatic diurnal temperature changes due to high elevation. Over ten times as many wineries enjoy these advantages now.

VINEYARD ELEVATION
Range: 1,300–1,800 feet.

WINES
Ceago Estate pictured below is located in the Clear Lake AVA. Situated right on the lake, it experiences no frost as a result of the lake's moderating influence. Sauvignon Blanc and Cabernet Sauvignon are the county's most famous varietals, but the sheer diversity of vineyard locations and soils has enabled a truly exciting range of excellent wine styles.

THE TERROIR/MESOCLIMATE
The interesting geology of this large AVA area has provided a wealth of different soil types, topographies, and mesoclimates. This AVA was orginally devised to encircle the traditional farmlands of the county, and indeed the valley floors are where many of the first vineyards were planted. The soils on the valley floors also vary but are often sandy loam and clay loam. The Big Valley and Upper Lake areas to the northwest are considerably cooler and drier than areas to the southern end of the county. The Ceago Estate (above), started by Jim Fetzer, enjoys the benefits of Clear Lake's "wind machine effect." The breezes from the lake enable an exciting range of varietals to grow in the adjoining hillside vineyards.

STILL LOAM /STRATIFIED SOIL

VARIETALS GROWN
SAUVIGNON BLANC • CHARDONNAY
SAUVIGNON MUSQUÈ • SEMILLION
MUSCAT CANELLI • CABERNET FRANC
CABERNET SAUVIGNON • MALBEC
SYRAH • PETIT VERDOT • MERLOT
PETITE SIRAH • TEMPRANILLO
PINOT NOIR • LENOIR • BARBERA
PETIT VERDOT

LAKE WINERIES
Olof Cellars

Red Hills AVA (2004)

Red Hills is perhaps *the* red-hot AVA in the region, but not because the underlying volcanics are restless again. This time it's the vineyards that are blanketing the hills, springing up everywhere. It is with good reason: visionary growers who planted vines here 30 years ago are finding their grapes are now highly sought after. The area has also attracted some of the world's best winemakers who are making wines that are astounding wine critics. Andy Beckstoffer, one of Napa's most prominent vineyard owners, believes that the area's Cabernet Sauvignon wine is "the most promising new wine in the New World of wines"–a lofty claim, but one that seems to be bearing fruit.

VINEYARD ELEVATION
Range: 1,400–3,000 feet.
Majority: 2,000-2,600 feet.

WINES
Notable AVA for producing big intense berry flavored reds, with deep color and complexity. Winemakers note earthy, minerally, "mountain fruit" flavors from the elevated volcanic soils. Cabernet Sauvignon leads the single varietals, but Petite Sirah, Malbec, Zinfandel, Grenache, Syrah, and Cabernet Franc also thrive here.

THE TERROIR/MESOCLIMATE

GLENVIEW-ARROWHEAD-COMPLEX/RED HILLS

Volcanic activity 1.5 million–10,000 years ago created the distinctive red soils. The main (parent material) soil types are: Aiken, formed on basalt; Soda Bay, on scoria; and Glenview-Arrowhead-Complex (left) on obsidian from rapidly cooled rhyolite; Bottle Rock, and Konocti. Soils are often deep, well-drained, and rocky and many have fragments of obsidian in them. These "mountain vineyards" have cold winters, dry hot summers, and a shorter growing season. Rapid diurnal temperature falls at night (often as much as 50˚F) create good acidity in grapes. Stronger UV light speeds up grape ripening times and causes thicker skins to form on the small concentrated berries. All this provides wines with greater intensity, color, tannins, and structure.

VARIETALS GROWN

CABERNET SAUVIGNON • SYRAH
CABERNET FRANC • GRENACHE
PETITE SIRAH • SYRAH • MERLOT
ZINFANDEL • MALBEC • MOUVÈDRE
PETIT VERDOT • SYRAH NOIR
COUNOISE • CINSAULT • CHARBONO

LAKE WINERIES

Thorn Hill • Gregory Graham
Sol Rouge • Obsidian Ridge
Hawk and Horse • Fore Family
Laujor Estate • Boatique Winery
Shannon Ridge Family of Wines

High Valley AVA (2005)

Utterly fascinating geologically, this AVA is a rare example of an east-west oriented fault basin in the Coastal Ranges. Sitting 300 feet above Clear Lake, this topographically isolated 8.5 mile long and 3 mile wide valley has a young volcanic cinder cone, Round Mountain, dividing the east and west portions. It is a viticulturist's and 'terroir-ista's dream', with its impressive array of Franciscan Complex, volcanic, and alluvial soils, along with steep mountain ridges and flat valley floors. Cool breezes from the lake below and nearby Mendocino National Forest get trapped inside the valley, which is key to the excellent quality and very interesting variety of wines produced here.

VINEYARD ELEVATION
Range: 1,700–3,000+ feet.

WINES
This AVA is a winemaker's playground as so many different varietals can thrive here. Due to the cooler weather, unusual varietals such as Pinot Noir, Pinot Grigio, Johannisberg Riesling, and Gewürztraminer can successfully be grown, making for some very interesting wines. The steep volcanic hillsides also provide the high quality "mountain" reds.

THE TERROIR/MESOCLIMATE
The valley was formed tectonically along with the Coastal Ranges and has Franciscan Complex hills to the southwest. The watershed originally drained eastward, then volcanic activity threw up a cinder cone which blocked off the valley and created a lake to the west. Now long gone, it has left behind deep alluvial soils on the valley floors (left). In the northeast, andesite and basalt volcanic ridges and soils dominate. Many vineyards are planted on the steep slopes of the valley at high elevation. This, plus the cool air that settles in the valley, is key in creating one of the coldest climates in the county, producing the prized "mountain fruit." The AVA has a very high water table and many natural springs. Vines close to 100 years old have been found here.

TALMAGE/CACHE CREEK

VARIETALS GROWN
SAUVIGNON BLANC • PINOT GRIS
GEWÜRZTRAMINER • RIESLING
CHARDONNAY • PINOT NOIR •
VIOGNIER • CABERNET SAUVIGNON
MERLOT • TEMPRANILLO • SYRAH
CABERNET FRANC • MOURVÈDRE
PETITE SIRAH • GRENACHE
ZINFANDEL • ZINFANDEL • MALBEC
PETIT VERDOT

LAKE WINERIES
Brassfield Estate Winery
Shannon Ridge Family of Wines

Big Valley District AVA (2013)

Big Valley's lush, flat land was the first area pioneer settlers identified as being ideal for farming back in the mid-1850s. Pre-Prohibition winemakers planted vineyards here before they later turned to pears and walnuts. The revival of winegrape growing in the 1960s began here, too. It took a few years to hone the balance between market trends and which grape varietals the terroir truly demanded. Sauvignon Blanc has won its place as one of *the* most popular varietals from this AVA. Deep soils deposited over millennia by the lake, brisk winds from surrounding hillsides, and cold air that sinks into the valley at night all provide the cool site for some even cooler wines.

VINEYARD ELEVATION

Range: 1,360–1,400 feet.

WINES

The hot daytime temperatures followed by much colder nights certainly seem to suit varietals such as Sauvignon Blanc particularly well. These conditions can provide some really lush tropical fruit flavors in the resulting wines. Great soils and welcome cooling off at night enable many varietals, both white and red, to excel on this prime farmland.

THE TERROIR/MESOCLIMATE

The valley is part of the structural basin that was formed when the Coastal Ranges were forming 2-3 million years ago. The soils are derived from Franciscan Complex and Great Valley Sequence parent materials, followed by millennia of lacustrine deposits and interwoven with volcanic debris from the adjacent Clear Lake Volcanic Field. This has left some very rich, deep soils. Cole clay loam, Clear Lake clay, and Still loam (left) are the most common. The valley is mostly flat with slopes of only 2-3° tilting very gently towards the lake. The very warm summer daytime temperatures are greatly mitigated by cool winds from surrounding hillsides, which can commence as early as mid-morning. Cold air that sinks into the valley means frost protection is nearly always needed here.

STILL SOIL/BIG VALLEY

VARIETALS GROWN

SAUVIGNON BLANC • RIESLING
CHARDONNAY • MUSCAT • SYRAH
MERLOT • ZINFANDEL • BARBERA
CABERNET SAUVIGNON • MERLOT
ZINFANDEL • NEBBIOLO • MALBEC
PETIT VERDOT • TEMPRANILLO

LAKE WINERIES

Chacewater • Steele Wines
Robledo Family • Aliénor Cellars
Wildhurst Vineyards • Kaz
Mt. Konocti Winery

Kelsey Bench AVA (2013)

As the name implies, this AVA sits a little higher than its Big Valley next door neighbor. If Big Valley is all about water and deposition, this AVA is all about uplift and volcanics. The Big Valley Fault (part of the San Andreas Fault system) sits below the Kelsey Bench, and the nature of this strike-slip fault has been to uplift these southern lands. The big San Francisco earthquake in 1906 apparently gave it an extra push up. Kelsey Bench gets its share of cool breezes to offset the hot summer days. These come from the high Mayacamas Mountains behind it. These breezes do not settle here, but keep on going down to the valley below, so that few grape growers in this AVA have to frost-protect their vines.

VINEYARD ELEVATION

Range: 1,400–1,600 feet.

WINES

Although a very close neighbor to Big Valley, Kelsey Bench winemakers have discovered that their somewhat different topography, soils, and climate are proving good sites for a number of red varietals, notably Cabernet Sauvignon, Petite Sirah, Merlot, and Zinfandel. No doubt others will emerge in this exciting AVA.

THE TERROIR/MESOCLIMATE

The Kelsey Bench was created between half to a quarter million years ago and is linked to the tectonic and volcanic activity that helped develop Clear Lake (see p.14). The area south of the Big Valley Fault is called the Kelseyville Formation and consists mainly of sandstone, siltstone, and mudstone. The majority of vineyards are planted on Manzanita-Wappo-Forbesville (left), the main soil type of the area. The soil tends to be found on milder slopes and is a deep, well-drained alluvial soil with a slight acidity. The somewhat "leaner" nature of these soils limits vine vigor and produces desirably more concentrated fruit. Two aquifers formed in volcanic deposits are important sources of water. Climatically, this AVA is warmer than Big Valley and cooler than the Red Hills AVAs.

FORBESVILLE SOIL/KELSEY BENCH

VARIETALS GROWN

PINOT GRIGIO • SAUVIGNON BLANC
MUSCATO • RIESLING • AGLIANICO
PINOT BLANC • SAGRANTINO
BARBERA • DOLCETTO • PRIMITIVO
NEBBIOLO • NEGROAMARO
REFOSCO • CABERNET SAUVIGNON

LAKE WINERIES

Rosa d'Oro Vineyards
Smiling Dogs Ranch

Wine Touring & Tasting in Lake County

OWNERS

Martin Pohl and Josef Rusnak

WINERY HISTORY

The vineyard was started in the early 1970s by the Horne family, who made wine on the property until 1995. In 2007 three partners from the Czech Republic took over the property and completely revived the vineyard, gaining organic and biodynamic certification.

WINEMAKER BIO

Martin Pohl, a Czech native, lived in Germany and Australia before immigrating to the US in 2001. He started out as a home winemaker, then got his permit in 2007. He and his partner are committed to making wine in as natural a way as possible, with no additives or chemicals used. The wines are handcrafted from beginning to end and are aged in French oak barrels.

ACREAGE / AVA

Horne ranch has a total of 22 acres under vine, Lake County Appellation.

ELEVATION

Average about 1,110 feet.

TERROIR / MICROCLIMATE

Middletown valley floor location. Very high temperature variations; hot during the day and cold at night. Ideal for organic farming as no sprays or emergents are used.

VARIETALS GROWN / ACREAGE

6 acres Sauvignon Blanc, 3 acres Petite Sirah, 12 acres Cabernet Sauvignon, with 1 acre Cabernet Franc grown for blending.

WINES PRODUCED

2,000 cases produced annually.

WINE CLUB

Wine club offers 4 bottles (usually 4 red) four times a year. Or you can choose 6 bottles, 4 red, 1 rosé, and 1 white. Members receive a 20% discount on wines.

Winemaking Philosophy

The winery is committed to the most highly sustainable farming practices and is CCOF organically certified and (since 2010) Demeter Certified Biodynamic. Martin believes that this careful tending of the soil is key to creating wines that are truly original: "Wines whose flavors and tastes come from the elements of nature."

This careful tending of the soil is matched with a very handcrafted winemaking process. The grapes are all hand-selected and harvested, have no additives and are all unfiltered. They are then aged in 10-20 percent new French oak barrels. The goal is to produce wines of the cleanest, purest quality that express the unique terroir of the site, wines where "Mother Nature is the senior winemaker."

Wine lovers who want to help promote the unity and balance between nature and humanity are particularly welcome visitors to this winery.

Opposite: Beaver Creek tasting room and picnic area.

Below: Sheep tending to their weed control and other duties.

Beaver Creek Vineyards

Beaver Creek is one of the very first wineries you encounter when driving north over Mt. St. Helena along Highway 29 from Calistoga. The vineyards are located along the wide, seasonal St. Helena Creek of the alluvial valley floor in Middletown.

The winery's goal of avoiding all chemical use is greatly assisted by the microclimate; big diurnal changes with especially hot daytime temperatures and cool evenings are hard on pests, and indeed no pesticides are used. This certified biodynamic and organic operation also uses a variety of sheep amongst the vines to provide natural weed control and fertilization.

Winemaker Martin Pohl and business partner/wine connoisseur Josef Rusnak both strive to produce unfiltered wines of the cleanest, purest quality. Their winemaking process is completely natural and they add only the absolute minimum amount of sulfites when necessary. Martin and Josef believe in a harmonious, low-impact farm operation where nature is completely respected.

ADDRESS
22000 Highway 29,
Middletown, CA 95461

CONTACT
707-987-1069
wine@beavercreekvineyards.com

TASTING ROOM
Open Fri-Sun 11 am–6 pm all year,
except January when closed.
Tasting fee policy $10 per person
or fee waived if $50 is spent.

FACILITIES
Picnic area. Dog friendly.

EVENTS
Occasional pick-up parties.
Lake County Wine Adventure
participant. BBQs and other events
advertised throughout the year.

OWNERS

Bob and Madi Mount

WINERY HISTORY

The Mounts have been interested in wine for many years, and purchased their property in the famous Red Hills AVA in 2011. They spent four years constructing the impressive winery.

WINEMAKER BIO

Sonoma County native, Patrick Sullivan, used his degree in Molecular Cell Biology in the Bio-Tech industry before entering the world of wine. He received a Masters Degree in Enology from CSU Fresno, and then worked for some prestigious Sonoma wineries, including 6 years as wine-maker for Rudd Winery, before becoming the consultant for Boatique.

ACREAGE / AVA

61 acres under vine. Red Hills AVA estate reds. Sauvignon Blanc grapes are from Big Valley AVA.

ELEVATION

Between 2,100-2,200 feet

TERROIR / MICROCLIMATE

Red Hills site: Well-drained, rocky volcanic red soil, mineral-rich containing obsidian. Typically hot, dry summer days, some cooling breezes from the lake and cool nights.

VARIETALS GROWN

Red Hills AVA reds include: 21 acres Petite Sirah, 14 acres Malbec, 4 acres Petit Verdot, 22 acres Cabernet Sauvignon. Sauvignon Blanc is grown in the Big Valley AVA.

WINES PRODUCED

300 cases Sauvignon Blanc, 250 cases Malbec Rosé, and an estimated 1,000 cases of various red varietals.

WINE CLUB

2 or 4 bottles quarterly with 15% or 20% discount to members. Complimentary tastings for 2 guests. Special events include themed pick-up parties, a Tulip Festival in Spring and popular "Women and Wine" events.

Winemaking Philosophy

Bob and Madi Mount were committed to producing the finest quality wines possible from their Red Hills AVA Vineyard site from the get-go. They invested in a state-of-the art winery, including an impressive row of concrete "eggs" which are a modern incarnation of an ancient winemaking technique. The history of these fascinating structures is on display alongside what must be one of the best collection of rare wooden boats anywhere, ensuring that a visit to Boatique is a feast for the eyes as well as the taste buds! The winery is a popular location for weddings and charitable events. Boatique winemaker Patrick Sullivan learned his craft at Peter Michael Winery, Lewis Cellars, Paul Hobbs and Rudd Winery in Napa and Sonoma Counties before starting his consultancy business. His many years of experience, dedication and hard work make him a perfect fit for the Boatique family. He is, in turn, excited to create more award-winning wines from such exceptional quality winegrapes.

Below: The Mounts with a classic 1950s Chris Craft boat

Boatique Winery ②

Bob and Madi Mount first opened their beautiful winery in the Red Hills AVA in May 2015. The couple are not newcomers to Lake County, however. For many years they brought their young family to the area for holidays, and enjoyed summers spent water-skiing on the Lake. When an opportunity presented itself to acquire a vineyard property in the county they jumped at the chance to put down roots in an area for which they had developed such a deep affection.

Boatique surely has a spectacular location, with panoramic views over Mount Konocti across the rolling hills of the famous Red Hills appellation–where some of the most highly-acclaimed wine in the county is being produced.

Boatique, as the name suggests, is also home to an incredible collection of antique and classic wooden boats. Bob Mount has been rescuing and lovingly restoring them for years. The boats date from the 1930s, and are truly amazing works of art, happily now on display for us all to enjoy.

ADDRESS
8255 Red Hills Road,
Kelseyville, CA 95451

CONTACT
707-279-2675
www.boatiquewines.com
nahani@boatiquewinery.com

TASTING ROOM
Open Daily 11 am–5 pm,
$5 tasting fee, waived with purchase.

FACILITIES
Tasting room is adjacent to the showroom for the antique & classic wooden boat collection. Picnic area, gardens, food available, gift shop,

EVENTS
Varied events include music, art, and entertainment. Tulip Festival in Spring. Club members' quarterly wine and food pairings, and in Summer, the 1st Monday of the month, wood-fired oven Pizza Nights with music. Wine Adventure Participant.

Winemaking Philosophy

Brassfield creates expressive wines that are an authentic reflection of the estate. Old World winemaking techniques such as native yeast fermentation allow true expression of the terroir. Sur lie aging with battonage (stirring) in small vessels enhances texture and body, and bottling without filtration preserves delicate aromas and flavors.

Respect for the land and a keen sense of stewardship have guided all of the winery's practices. Farming is guided by quality over quantity, favoring low crop yields to intensify fruit. Meticulous grooming ensures optimal sun exposure to achieve physiological ripeness. Grapes are harvested pre-dawn using gentle methods so that the fruit arrives at the crush pad in pristine condition.

Opposite: A jewel in the landscape: Brassfield Visitors Center is set amongst golden hills and sparkling vistas.

Below: Magnificent creatures roam free on the Wildlife Preserve.

Brassfield Estate Winery ③

The large nearly 3,000-acre Brassfield Estate is set in a breathtaking natural location. Owner Jerry Brassfield, mindful of the very special nature of the property, has set aside 1,000 acres of the land for a wildlife preserve. The High Valley AVA was formed, like much of Lake County, by intense volcanic activity. Round Mountain Volcano, which sits at the eastern end of the east-west oriented valley, erupted just 10,000 years ago. It formed a dam that has kept successive layers of volcanic and alluvial materials trapped inside it.

The valley floor is 1,800 feet above sea level, and surrounding ridges and hillsides rise to nearly 3,000 feet. There are an amazingly large number of different microclimates, allowing for a wide range of grape varietals to thrive. Proximity to the lake enables cold air to be sucked into the valley, such that up to a 50-degree diurnal temperature change is possible. The High Valley floor is one of the few locations in Lake County that is cool enough to grow great Pinot Noir.

ADDRESS
10915 High Valley Road,
Clearlake Oaks, CA 95423

CONTACT
707-998-1895
www.brassfieldestate.com
info@brassfieldestate.com

TASTING ROOM
Open Daily 10 am–5 pm
$10 tasting fee for 5 tastes.

FACILITIES
Stunning visitors center and tasting room, picnic area, farm to bottle vineyard cave tours, and corporate events. Tours by appointment.

EVENTS
Many and varied wine club events, from frequent new release parties to Murder Mystery dinners and the popular Summer Eruption party. Participant In Wine Adventure.

Winemaking Philosophy

Bullion Creek Vineyards, on the northern slopes of Mt. St. Helena, is close to the historic site of Robert Louis Stevenson's mountain refuge. Stevenson famously said "Wine is bottled poetry." Richard Brand was also attracted to the quiet beauty of this place. Plus he hoped his young son might enjoy the adventure, and sheer hard work, of starting a vineyard. That idea seems to have paid off as his son now works in the wine industry. Richard is very much guided by nature in his winemaking. "We grow bottles of wine," he declares on his web site. His harvest time is guided by the birds; if they start picking on his Chardonnay grapes, then he knows it's time to harvest.

He irrigates with pure water, that was once bottled and sold, from an old artesian well. He custom crushes his wine at Mt. Konocti Growers in Kelseyville. Richard's driving goal is to make great wine "no matter how long it takes," so he does not rush his wines and he lets them age an average of 20 months before bottling.

Opposite & Below: Lines of Cabernet vines, well-versed in lofty composition.

Bullion Creek Vineyards 4

Originally from Bakersfield in the San Joaquin Valley in Southern California, Richard Brand has worked across the state. His working life is an interesting blend of engineering and farming. He was one of the first to be involved in the wind turbine business. He discovered Lake County when he came to be a "Mud Engineer" working at The Geysers in the 1970s, also an industry in its early days. He was instantly attracted to what he describes as the "pristine" nature of the environment here, and Lake County has, for some time, earned the prestigious "cleanest air in the nation" accolade.

Attracted to this beautiful rural community of just 45,000 inhabitants–"Back then you could lay down on 29," (the highway to the town of Calistoga 15 miles away)–he decided to buy property on the north slopes of Mt. St. Helena. His former turbine partner, a wine buff, sparked an idea in him to try winemaking. So he planted Cabernet and found people at the Napa Wine Club wanted to know why his wine was so good. Great soil, pure water, and take your time, he'd likely say.

ADDRESS
24073 Highway 29,
Middletown, CA 95461
Mail:
P.O. BOX 741
Middletown, CA 95461

CONTACT
707-535-6970, 707-987-9244
www.bullioncreekvineyards.com
Follow on Twitter and Facebook
bullioncreek@yahoo.com

TASTING ROOM
By appointment.
No tasting fee with wine purchase.

FACILITIES
Tasting in the vineyard available by appointment.

EVENTS
Participant in Lake County Wine Adventure.

OWNERS

The Van Pelt Family

WINERY HISTORY

Bill "Poppo" Van Pelt purchased a 590-acre parcel on Cache Creek in 1997, with a vision of creating a wildlife sanctuary for Tule elk and other native wildlife. Today that dream is realized, along with 74 acres of vineyards.

WINEMAKER BIO

Derek Holstein, a well-renowned consulting winemaker, has made Cache Creek's wines since the first vintage. His deep knowledge of Lake County terroir and grapes comes from years of working closely with Beckstoffer Vineyards, and as wine-maker for 12 years at Guenoc.

ACREAGE / AVA

Over 74 acres of sustainably farmed vineyards are planted in Lake County.

ELEVATION

Average 1,200 feet.

TERROIR / MICROCLIMATE

In the growing season, daily tempera-ture swings of 35° F+ help preserve bright acidity in the grapes. The mostly rocky gravel and loam soil gets an annual average rainfall of 30 inches, which is channeled into a series of ponds which are used for irrigation and also to support wildlife.

VARIETALS GROWN

Cabernet Sauvignon, Petite Sirah, Syrah, Chardonnay, and Sauvignon Blanc.

WINES PRODUCED

They produce 3,000 cases annually. 100% estate grown single-vineyard wines: Cabernet Sauvignon, Petite Sirah, Syrah, Chardonnay, Sauvignon Blanc. Also a rosé, sparkling wine, a white blend, and a dessert wine.

WINE CLUB

Two clubs with discounts ranging from 15-25%. Mixed, white only, or red only options. Additional 5% off by-the-case purchases during your birthday month. Pick-up parties with food pairings.

Winemaking Philosophy

Derek Holstein, a man of many talents, is a musician as well as a winemaker. His view of winemaking reflects the range of his artistic interests. "Fine wine is an art form for me, lending me the privilege of creative expression. It enriches and inspires my life, and I endeavor to spread that inspiration from farm to table." Derek compares his winemaker role to that of an orchestra conductor. He works with every member of the team (his orchestra), including owner Don Van Pelt and vineyard foreman Tony Medina, to refine their sustainable farming practices and strive to continuously produce premium quality grapes. In the cellar, under Derek's guidance, the wine-making team produces harmonious compositions year after year. The proof is an ever-growing list of awards, and the many regular visitors.

Opposite: A perfect place to bring a picnic—close to the tasting room.

Below: The beautifully designed new winery has a spectacular natural setting, with many outdoor event spaces, and is a popular music and wedding venue.

Cache Creek's creatively designed winery, located just off Hwy 20, at the northeastern edge of Lake County, will likely be the first stop for wine-lovers visiting from the Sacramento Valley. Fittingly it superbly showcases all that is special about this rural, less-commercialized wine country. Few wineries can offer a sight of rare Tule elk, while you sip on a fine wine, in a 590-acre wilderness–this one can.

The vision for this lovely winery and wildlife sanctuary came from the late Bill Van Pelt, father and grandfather to the current owners. He purchased the land because he fell in love with the beauty, the natural environment and the wildlife, including a large herd of Tule elk, that roam freely through the property. From the beginning, a commitment to the land inspired the Van Pelts to sustainably farm the land and preserve the property as a wildlife habitat.

In the summer of 2017, the vineyards were recognized as Certified California Sustainable Winegrowers by the California Sustainable Winegrowing Alliance. The wines and location are an uplifting blend.

ADDRESS
250 New Long Valley Road, Clearlake Oaks, CA 95423
Mail: P.O. Box 1250, Clearlake Oaks, CA 95423

CONTACT
707-998-1200
www.cachecreekvineyards.com
info@cachecreekvineyards.com

TASTING ROOM
Open Daily 10.30 am–5.30 pm
$5 tasting fee, waived with purchase.

FACILITIES
Tasting room with gift shop, well-stocked deli case, picnic grounds, bocce court, views of Cache Creek, RV parking, and pet-friendly area. Available for private events of all sizes including weddings.

EVENTS
Many events including a summer concert series. *See website*.

OWNERS

Paul and Kellye Manuel

WINERY HISTORY

Paul and Kellye were successful grape growers in the Sierra Foothills before buying a 10-acre olive orchard and mill from the monks of St. Gregory Monastery in Kelseyville in 2008. They added a large winery and had their first release in 2011.

WINEMAKER BIO

This is very much a family business. Paul Manuel and son Matt are very hands-on at every stage of the winemaking process. Matt, who has a degree in Agricultural Business from Purdue University, ensures that their organically farmed Ponderosa Vineyards supply the finest quality grapes.

ACREAGE / AVA

50% of fruit used is from 36 acres in their Sierra Foothills vineyards. The other 50% is from a variety of Lake County growers in differing AVAs.

ELEVATION

Average about 1,950 feet.

TERROIR / MICROCLIMATE

A wide variety of soils and micro-climates both in the Sierra Foothills and throughout Lake County.

VARIETALS GROWN

From Sierra Foothills: Cabernet Sauvignon, Cabernet Franc, Merlot, Syrah, Zinfandel. From Lake County: Sauvignon Blanc, Chardonnay, Riesling, Merlot, Malbec, Petite Sirah, and a Cabernet Sauvignon from the Bartolucci Vineyards in Red Hills AVA.

WINES PRODUCED

11,000 cases of wine, and 2,000 cases of olive oil annually. A large range of varietals in both.

WINE CLUB

There are wine only, olive oil only, or wine and olive oil club memberships. 20% discount on all wine or olive oil and a 30% discount on all case sales. New release priority, plus many excellent and well-attended club events.

Winemaking Philosophy

Chacewater Winery & Olive Mill is a true family concern. The family's remarkably strong work-ethic (which they attribute to their Cornish mining roots) has seen them turn a devastating fire into a golden opportunity. Paul and Kellye Manuels' decision to plant vines on their land after a fire cleared it 30 years ago–has proven to be a very good one. Paul had previously run multi-million dollar construction projects, but felt those mining roots drawing him back to the land, and that somehow his "blood and spirit" were "firmly rooted in the earth." The love-of-land gene has been passed down to the next generation (of three boys who grew up playing and working in the vineyards). Matt the youngest son, who was born the same month the first vines were planted, is now a passionate organic farmer. He manages the family's Ponderosa Vineyards, ensuring winegrapes of exceptional quality–proven by their many award-winning wines. The Manuels' also source fruit from carefully selected local growers. Their 2014 "*Nell Cabernet Sauvignon Red Hills Lake County*" won an impressive 93 point score from the *Wine Enthusiast*.

Opposite: Chacewater Syrah vineyards sunbathing in the Sierra Foothills. Below: Sample an impressive selection of olive oils in the tasting room.

Chacewater Winery & Olive Mill **6**

Paul and Kellye Manuel's roots both go back to Cornwall, England. The Cornish were excellent tin miners, and Paul's great-grandfather brought this expertise to the Gold Country. On a visit to the family church in the village of Chacewater, a mason's mark caught Paul's eye. This is now their logo, to honor their Cornish roots and pioneering spirit.

Paul worked in the family's construction business on 80 acres outside of Nevada City. When a devastating fire in 1988 swept through the land, clearing it, he decided to see if he could grow grapes. In 1988 they put in their first 10 acres and earned a reputation for the exceptional quality of their organically grown fruit. They expanded to 36 acres, selling fruit to big wineries such as Fetzer. In 2004 they tried a custom crush in Lake County and sold it as bulk wine. In 2008 they purchased a 10-acre olive farm and mill from a local monastery and built a 10,000 sq. ft. winery next to the mill. A county superstar, they rapidly progressed from their first release in 2011 to being the "Golden State Winery of the Year in 2012."

ADDRESS
5625 Gaddy Lane,
Kelseyville, CA 95451

CONTACT
707-279-2995
www.chacewaterwine.com

TASTING ROOM
Open Daily 11 am–5 pm
Taste any 7 wines for $5 fee,
with complimentary olive oil tasting,
if desired. Guided tours available.

FACILITIES
Picnic area in large covered crush pad overlooking olive trees. Bocce ball court and horseshoe pits.

EVENTS
Seasonal pick-up parties, Kelseyville Olive Oil Festival, participant in Lake County Wine Adventure. Fall harvest party.

OWNERS
Miguel and Lupita Silva

WINERY HISTORY
After working in the Lake County wine industry for over 23 years, Miguel Silva wanted to make his own wines. He released his first wines in 2012 and he and wife Lupita decided to open a tasting room on Main Street in Lakeport in 2014.

WINEMAKER BIO
Miguel was the former Cellar Master and Assistant Winemaker at Steele Wines before joining Mt. Konocti Winery in 2004, which he left in 2015 to focus on his own brand of wines.

ACREAGE / AVA
Don Angel Cellars sources grapes from many different growers, approximately 80% of whom are in the county of Lake. At present a small proportion of grapes come from the adjoining counties of Napa and Sonoma, but he is transitioning to be 100% Lake County-sourced grapes.

ELEVATION
Various: from 1,300-2,600.

TERROIR / MICROCLIMATE
Various: all North Coast AVA grown.

WINES PRODUCED
300-400 cases produced annually. Sauvignon Blanc, Chardonnay, Viognier, Montepulciano, Malbec, Sangiovese, Petite Sirah, Zinfandel, Cabernet Sauvignon. He also makes "Lupita's Blend," a Sangiovese and Pinot Noir blend named after his wife. Miguel enjoys making dessert wines; he has made a Petite Sirah that resembles a port, and has released some white dessert wines, an Orange Muscat and a Muscat Cannelli.

WINE CLUB
The wine club offers different levels of membership, from 6-24 bottles annually. Customer's choice of available wines. A 20% discount on all wine sales. Advance notice of special offers and Don Angel Cellars events.

Winemaking Philosophy

Like many in this book, Miguel also firmly believes that great wines are made in the vineyard, and he certainly recognizes and appreciates good quality grapes. It is what happens inside the winery, however, that particularily seems to excite him– the potential to take that fruit and turn it into something special. His philosophy is that wines should be "grounded," and he has a motto for his winemaking style which is "uncomplicated and delicious." He wants his wines to be approachable and not at all intimidating.

He is clearly enjoying the liberty of creating his own wines. He has had some early critical success, too: his 2010 Lake Cabernet Sauvignon received a gold in the *San Froncoisco Chronicle* awards. Having been around for a while he is occasionally offered fruit from less well-known varietals, and he welcomes the chance to experiment with this. Look out for some interesting new releases from a steady pair of hands now with the freedom to play.

Opposite: "Don" Miguel Angel Silva. Below: Lupita Silva pouring their wine.

Miguel Silva and wife Lupita are the very friendly owners who will most likely greet you at Don Angel Cellars. But don't ask for Don! "Don Angel" is a name that spoke to Miguel as he was trying to decide what to call his new wine brand. The "Don" part is an homage to his Mexican roots (an honorary, respectful way of addressing elders), Angel is his middle name, which seemed to bolt together nicely with Don and has made a very attractive wine label.

Miguel has a long history with the Lake County wine industry, and his story is a right place, right time one. In the 1990s he came to work for Myron Holdenried in his vineyards. Myron later offered Miguel a position at the Wildhurst Winery. At Wildhurst he met Kathy McGrath, a South African born consultant winemaker, under whose guidance Miguel came to really love the art of winemaking. In 1996 he moved to work with Jed Steele in Kelseyville as his cellar master. He was made assistant winemaker at Steele in 2002. In 2004 he became winemaker for Mt. Konocti Winery (on the historic Mt. Konocti Growers site). In 2015 he left Mt. Konocti to concentrate on his own Don Angel Cellars wines.

ADDRESS
165 North Main Steet,
Lakeport, CA 95453

CONTACT
707-349-6312
www.donangelcellars.com

TASTING ROOM
Open Wed-Sat 11 am–5 pm
$4 tasting fee, refunded with purchase.

FACILITIES
The nicely decorated tasting room right on Main Street has wall space dedicated to changing art exhibitions.

EVENTS
There are plans to host food and wine pairing events emphasizing the flavors and foods of Mexico. Contact the tasting room for details. Participant in Wine Adventure.

OWNERS

Jim and Diane Fore

WINERY HISTORY

Jim and Diane bought the 40-acre parcel of land in Red Hills AVA in 2000. Their first Lake County vintage was a 2005 Cabernet, Syrah, and Grenache Noir blend. They only make wines from grapes they farm themselves.

WINEMAKER BIO

Jim Fore, son Eric, and Winemaker Tim Dolven all help create the wines. The art and craft of winemaking is emphasized, as is the desire to produce wines and blends exclusively from their own fruit.

ACREAGE / AVA

17 acres in Lake County Red Hills AVA and 35 acres farmed in Napa.

ELEVATION

Cobb Mountain 3,000+ feet

TERROIR / MICROCLIMATE

Red varietals grown on Lake County volcanic Red Hills soils with cool nights and snow possible in winter.

VARIETALS GROWN

Lake County: Cabernet Sauvignon, Mouvèdre, Zinfandel, Grenache Noir, Grenache Blanc, Syrah.
Napa: Sauvignon Blanc, Albariño, Pinot Noir, Merlot.

WINES PRODUCED

1,000 cases produced annually. Single varietal wines, listed above. plus their award-winning "G.S.M", a blend of Grenache, Syrah and Mouvèdre.

WINE CLUB

Wine ships to club members 3 times per year. The commitment is 2, 4, 6 or 12 bottles per year which can be red, white or mixed. Members receive a 15% discount on all wine purchases. Many free wine club events and parties, complimentary wine tastings anytime for up to two people.

Winemaking Philosophy

The general philosophy of Fore Family Vineyards is to "grow the finest winegrapes possible using sustainable techniques and values acknowledging that we are transient stewards of the land." Jim Fore, son Eric, and Winemaker Tim Dolven, all adhere to that philosophy. As well as producing the grapes for their own wines, they also supply many others with fruit, including some very well-known brands.

Winemaker Tim Dolven hails from Bethel, Maine. After college in Ohio, he moved to Napa in 1985, and has been working in the wine industry ever since. His knowledge of all aspects of winemaking was learned in many diverse winery posts. He was assistant winemaker at Honig, Havens, and Franus, progressing to be the Winemaker at Stelzner and Bouchaine. He joined Fore Family in 2013 and loves the opportunity to really embrace the Art of winemaking. This is what Jim calls the "fun part" crafting wines that really showcase each unique varietal.

Opposite: The tasting room offers a large selection of wines to try.
Below: Gus the winery dog enjoying the snow in the vineyard.

Fore Family Vineyards 8

Jim Fore was an engineer draftsman for navy submarines in Vallejo. In 1994 the shipyard was closed and that brought a chance for Jim and wife Diane to opt for a totally different lifestyle. Jim, a Napa native, was a keen hobby winemaker, and had achieved considerable success in local competitions with friends out of a garage winery.

In 1995 he teamed up with Doug Hill, a Napa grape-grower, to produce quality wine grapes. In 2000 they started their own vineyard. Jim considered other wine regions, but knew that Lake County had great soils and climate. The property on Cobb Mountain was found by an old friend. On his first visit to the site Jim thought "You have to be crazy to farm here."

They are some of the highest vines in the county and are producing exceptional fruit. The interesting choice of varietals grown on their 17-acre site is producing a great selection of wines and blends to try. Son Eric joined the business in 2014, and they have plans to expand further, eventually producing a wine for each of the 13 varietals they grow.

ADDRESS
3924 Main Street,
Kelseyville, CA 95451

CONTACT
707-287-3955
www.forewines.com
diane@forefamilyvineyards.com

TASTING ROOM
Open Friday–Sunday 11 am–5 pm
$5 for 5 pours. Fee waived with a
bottle purchase.

FACILITIES
Large tasting room and event space.
Rotating display of local artists' and
photographers' work. Musical concerts. Available for private hire.

EVENTS
Sip 'n' Paint parties. Vertical Cabernet
tastings, monthly art receptions.
Open for Kelseyville Olive and Pear
Festivals and all town events.
Wine Adventure Participant.

OWNERS
Kendall Fults and Dustin Fults

WINERY HISTORY

Kendall Fults bought the 45-acre ranch in 2001, and planted the first block of vines on the property in 2005. His son Dustin moved to the ranch in 2005, and proposed that he and his father start a family winery together. In 2014 the Fults Family Vineyards tasting room was built. The first vintage and official Grand Opening was in 2015.

WINEMAKER BIO

There was always a family passion for winemaking, and Kendall, Dustin and his uncle Cecil Lamerton made wine as a hobby in Napa for many years. Dustin studied Viticulture at Napa College, and also achieved a Level 2 Sommelier qualification. Help from long-time friend Eric Stine (a former colleague at Langtry) has further honed Dustin's skills as the Fults Family Vineyards winemaker.

ACREAGE / AVA

4 acres under vine, 12 more planned.

ELEVATION

Average 1,700 feet.

TERROIR / MICROCLIMATE

Soils are mostly silty clay-loam.

VARIETALS GROWN

Cabernet Sauvignon, Petite Sirah, Petit Verdot, Malbec, Grenache, Sangiovese, Sauvignon Blanc, Moscato, and Pinot Gris.

WINES PRODUCED

Some unique 100% estate blends: "Super Tuscan" and "Twilight" (red) and "Grace" (white). Many other single varietal wines, a Blanc de Blanc sparkling wine, and another great red blend called "Wildfire."

WINE CLUB

Wine club membership is 6 bottles twice a year, can be red only or mixed. The popular 100% estate blends are reserved for members.

Winemaking Philosophy

Kendall Fults, a native of Nebraska originally, discovered Lake County in 2001 when he was appointed CEO of a local hospital. He fell in love with the landscape, and soon purchased a 45-acre parcel ranch between Lower Lake and Middletown. A family passion for winemaking found him planting a small block of vines soon after. When work called Kendall to the Central Valley, his son Dustin came to care-take the ranch. With great serendipity, Dustin's first employment in the county was for the Langtry Estate Winery, where he was quickly immersed in all aspects of the wine business. Importantly, he also made a great personal friendship with the winemaker Eric Stine, now of industry-wide stature. When Dustin pitched the idea of starting a family winery on the ranch to his dad in 2008, happily "he didn't take much persuading." Much hard work ensued in constructing the winery. A mix of great passion for wine, plus some generous advice from talented friends like Eric Stine, has ensured that the wines are turning out to be just chipper.

Opposite: The Chip-Shot green—just a hole-in-one from the winery.
Below: The relaxing winery terrace overlooking the lake.

Fults Family Vineyards

9

An extra 'F' could well be added to the "FFV" Fults Family Vineyards logo–as their motto "Friends, Family and Fun"–is evident from when you first arrive at their welcoming tasting room. A large barrel of golf balls, just outside, dares you to try for a hole-in-one on the "Chip-Shot" course next to the lake. Father and son team Kendall and Dustin Fults do a great job at making you feel like part of their extended family.

Dustin points out that some of the labels even have his grandmother's handwriting on them. It is clear that this close family loves to share what they do so well–and that is make great wine and host some very memorable events.

Plans to expand the vineyards with some new varietals are underway (so hopefully there are more interesting estate blends to come). They generously encourage people to walk through the property, and plan to enable some fishing also. Lots more fun to be had, no doubt, but the real ace-in-the-hole is a glass of their fine wine on the terrace!

ADDRESS
11441 Highway 29,
Lower Lake, CA 95457

CONTACT
707-690-0338
www.ffvwines.com
info@ffvwines.com

TASTING
Open Thur–Sun 11 am–5 pm,
and in Winter 12 pm–5 pm.
By appointment rest of week.
Tasting fee $5 waived with purchase.

FACILITIES
Terrace, picnics welcome, cheese and snacks available. Dog-friendly. Walking trails; Chip-Shot course. Winery and terrace are available for rent for private parties.

EVENTS
Participant in Lake County Wine Adventure. Pick-up parties in November and May. Annual Chip-Shot tournament.

Winemaking Philosophy

Greg is very committed to sustainable practices and has completed the self-assessment workshops for both the vineyard and winery. Since 2011 the winery has been 100% solar powered. His hands-on vineyard management is accompanied by precision timing of the harvest followed by "small lot" winemaking techniques. "Wines are made in the vineyard and harvest should take place at the optimum moment – not when dictated by a schedule," he believes.

Greg is firmly rooted in the more artisanal winemaking tradition. Single varietals are typically crafted to be bright and fruit forward and these wines have a strong local following. The Grahams' love of Rhône blends, discovered on their honeymoon, is reflected in the Syrah-based *Cinder Cone Reserve*. Greg's daughter Lisa is a chef, which shows in delicious and unique seasonal food and wine pairings offered at club parties and the Lake County Wine Adventure.

Opposite: Grapes hang on the vine waiting for the final harvest date.
Below: Greg and Marianne stroll down Crimson Hill with their dogs.

Gregory Graham Wines

10

Gregory Graham's family in Ohio farmed Concord grapes, so maybe caring for grapes is in his DNA. With a background in engineering, a degree in Enology and over 15 years' experience as a winemaker at two prestigious Napa Valley wineries, he was ready to embark on his own vineyard and winery project.

Greg and Marianne began looking at a location for their endeavor. Greg was impressed by the unique climate and soils of Lake County, and believed the area had great potential for producing high-quality wine grapes. The volcanic soils in the Red Hills AVA are ideally suited for the Rhône varietals Greg wanted to grow.

When the Grahams moved to Lake County in 2000, there were a number of vineyards but only a handful of wineries. They saw the opportunity to get in on the "ground floor" of an up-and-coming wine region, and they are seeing their vision realized. Visitors are warmly welcomed to come and taste their many award-winning wines in their cozy tasting room.

ADDRESS
13633 Point Lakeview Road,
Lower Lake, CA 95457

CONTACT
707-995-3500
www.ggwines.com
info@ggwines.com

TASTING ROOM
Open Fri-Sun 11 am–5 pm
and by appointment. $10 tasting fee,
waived with purchase.

FACILITIES
Picnic area, hiking trail between
Gregory Graham and Shannon Ridge-
Family of Wines (Vigilance Vineyards)
close by. The"Crimson Hill" guest
house on the property, that sleeps
eight, is available to rent through
VRBO, #317086.

EVENTS
Spring and fall club parties. Participant
in Lake County Wine Adventure and
"Barrels & Verticals."

WINERY HISTORY

Founded in 1999 by David Boies, Tracey Hawkins, and Mitch Hawkins on the historic Diamond B Ranch, at El Roble Grande in Lower Lake. The ranch dates back to stagecoach days. Their first release was in 2004.

WINEMAKER BIO

A native of California's wine country, Tracey grew up in Sonoma County, where wine was a natural part of life. When the family purchased the property in Lake County, her vision of an estate vineyard was kindled. In 1999 she launched Hawk and Horse Vineyards and continues to collaborate with consulting wine-maker, Dr. Richard Peterson.

ACREAGE / AVA

Total of 24 acres under vine in the Red Hills and North Coast AVAs.

ELEVATION

Between 1,800–2,200 feet.

TERROIR / MICROCLIMATE

Rocky, red volcanic soils consisting of Aiken, Collayomi and Whispering loam. Artesian springs and 3 small lakes on site water the vines. Lake County "diamonds" found on the site are used in biodynamic preparations.

VARIETALS GROWN

15 acres Cabernet Sauvignon, 3 acres each Cabernet Franc, Petit Verdot, and Petite Sirah.

WINES PRODUCED

2,500 cases produced annually. 100% estate grown.

WINE CLUB

Membership levels: 6 or 12 bottles shipped 3 times a year. Exclusive access to limited release and library reserve wines, plus a complimentary tour of ranch and vineyards once a year for 4 guests.

Winemaking Philosophy

The Hawk and Horse winemaking philosophy is very much that "wine is made in the vineyard." The land is biodynamically farmed due to a firm belief that by employing farming practices which are in harmony with nature, "a wine of beauty, which is expressive of our very special vineyard site" can be made. Many of the materials needed for biodynamic protocols are sourced on site. A herd of Scottish Highland cattle add to the diversity and sustainability. Lake County diamonds found on site are the exact form of silica used in biodynamic preparation 501 or "Horn Silica." Old World winemaking practices are used in the cel-lar. The winemaking team employs a very hands-on, careful, attention-to-details approach with minimal intervention and uses 100% French oak barrels. Their aim is to make wines that are elegant, full-bodied, food-friendly, and that truly reflect the site. "A wine of authenticity from our diamond-studded, spring-fed volcanic soils to your glass."

Opposite: The mountain vineyard planted to Cabernet Sauvignon.
Below: Other Lake County jewels found at harvest time.

Hawk and Horse Vineyards

When owner David Boies found the historic El Roble Grande Ranch in Lower Lake back in 1982, he knew he had found the perfect property to realize his dream for a vineyard of world-class distinction. The historic horse ranch had a rustic elegance, but most importantly the land was spectacular. Today the ranch encompasses 1,300 acres of some of the most pristine wildlands in California.

Mitch and Tracey Hawkins took over the daily operations of the ranch in 1999 and planned the biodynamic vineyard operation. The vines were planted in 2001 and the first release, the 2004, was met with an International Gold Medal.

The family maintains the original ranch feel of the property. The tasting room, in a part of the former horse trainer's residence, is kept as a tack room with antique saddles and memorabilia from the property's storied past. American Saddlebred and Quarter Horses share the land with hawks and the Scottish Highland cattle herd.

ADDRESS
13048 Highway 29
Lower Lake, CA 95457
Mail: P.O. Box 11
Lower Lake, CA 95457

CONTACT
707-942-4600
www.hawkandhorsevineyards.com
tracey@hawkandhorsevineyards.com

TASTING ROOM
Open by appointment and
weekends 11 am–4:30 pm
Tasting fee $10 per person.
$45 for extended ranch and vineyard
tour, includes tasting.

FACILITIES
Picnic area available for customers.

EVENTS
Wine Society (wine club) annual
Harvest Party, participant in Lake
County Wine Adventure.

OWNER

Richard "Kaz" Kasmier

WINERY HISTORY

In 2016 he began producing wine under his new Lakeport Winery label with locally sourced fruit.

WINEMAKER BIO

After a successful career as an advertising photographer and 8 years as an award-winning amateur winemaker, Richard Kasmier entered the world of commercial winemaking. Among other positions, he was a "cellar rat" at Wellington Winery. He purchased the property in Kenwood in 1986, planted 2.5 acres, and was granted a bond in 1994. His first release was made at Wellington Winery. After 20 years in Kenwood, he found his way to Lake County and is now operating Kaz Winery, Bodega Bay Portworks, and Lakeport Winery.

ACREAGE / AVA

All grapes sourced in Lake County. mostly from organic growers.

ELEVATION

Between 1,400 and 2,200 feet

WINES PRODUCED

500 cases a year. Single varietal wines: Sauvignon Blanc, Syrah, Petite Sirah, Pinot Noir, Barbera, Lenoir, Zinfandel. Red blends: Cabernet Sauvignon, Merlot, Petite Sirah, and Zinfandel; Merlot and Pinot Noir; Cabernet and Petit Verdot; plus a wide range of dessert wines: white ports, blush ports, ruby rose dessert wine, and tawny dessert wine.

WINE CLUBS

There are a number of different levels of membership in the wine club (Kaz Klub). They ship 3 times a year, Winter, Spring & Fall, with a minimum of 3 bottles at a time. A popular Port Club is also available. There are Several discounts available from 20% up to 30% for 12 or more bottles. Sign up in tasting room or on-line at www.kazwinery.com.

Winemaking Philosophy

Richard Kasmier is committed to making wine as purely as possible, from the vineyard to the glass. He describes his approach as "minimalist." He sources organic grapes (or as near-as), and then ferments them using no sulfites, no acids, no fining agents, or any other chemicals. He believes that Lake County grapes are so good they don't need "other stuff" added to them to make quality wine. Although 'Kaz' Kasmier has been making wine this way for decades, the rising interest in "Natural Wines" makes these highly individual wines very on-trend and captures the Zeitgeist towards purer, simpler products (and typically small-lot artisanal suppliers) free of the many additives often used for big-brand consistency.

Kaz hand-selects from the wide range of grape varietals grown in Lake County, sometimes buying as little as one row of grapes – but that row is carefully chosen. The wines are then crushed, aged, and bottled by hand at the Kaz/Lakeport Winery facility just outside the City of Lakeport. The whole family is involved in the business, and son Ryan creates the beautiful, quirky, retro labels.

Opposite: Kaz demonstrates siphoning straight from the barrel. Guests are encouraged to refill wine bottles and to create their own blends. Below: He supplies cool labels and pens to personalize your own blend.

Kaz / Lakeport Winery  12

Richard "Kaz" Kasmier owned a winery in Sonoma County for 20 years, before relocating to Lake County in 2015. He brought with him the wide variety of (very cool looking) "Kaz" labels, plus the popular "Bodega Bay Portworks." He is now adding a "Lakeport Winery" label to his repertoire, fittingly, as all of his wines are now made in county, and he has a very impressive range of port and dessert wines. He creates "good, easy drinking" wines for the Lakeport Winery label, and reserves the Kaz label for higher-end, best-of-year, small release wines and unusual blends. All grapes are sourced in county, and include some unusual varietals. His Lenoir wine is "good with bear"!

He offers a Blush Port (Nebbiolo), two White Ports (Sauvignon Blanc and Chardonnay) and a Primitivo Port. The Tawny Dessert Wine is a more traditional, Portuguese-style port, lighter, aged in-barrel for four or more years, and less syrupy than some California-style ports. For those curious about the new "Natural Wine" trend, Kaz is a must-visit destination, as he has been making wine with absolutely minimal intervention for years and produces some very unique wines.

ADDRESS
1435 Big Valley Road,
Lakeport, CA 95453

CONTACT
707-833-2536
kaz@kazwinery.com
www.kazwinery.com

TASTING ROOM
Open Saturday (only) 11 am–5 pm
and by appointment for groups.
Tasting fee $5 for 5 tastes, waived
with purchase.

FACILITIES
Picnic area, an innovative "self-fill",
"self-blend" program where you can
create your own unique wine.

EVENTS
A variety of seasonal events such as
"Summer Sangria Saturdays," "Barrels
& Verticals," and "Red White & Blues."
Wine Adventure participant. See web
site and Facebook for more.

OWNERS

Foley Family Wines and Malulani Investments, LLC

WINERY HISTORY

Actress Lillie Langtry, born on Jersey in the British Channel Islands, purchased the land in 1888 and planted vines over many acres. Langtry thought that the acreage was "paradise" and developed an elegant house and ranch buildings. She held the property for 18 years and claimed her Claret was the "finest in America." It is the first and largest winery in the county, now 23,000 acres. The winery has changed hands a number of times, most recently in 2012.

WINEMAKER BIO

Walter Jorge gained a degree in Agricultural Engineering from Zaragoza University, a degree in Oenology from the University of Rioja, then studied Oenology at the University of Montpellier in the Erasmus program. He came to California in 2008 to add "New World" winemaking skill to his very broad experience. He joined Langtry in 2017.

ACREAGE / AVA

Total of 450 acres under vine in Napa Valley, Guenoc Valley, and North Coast AVAs.

ELEVATION

Between 800-1,800 feet.

TERROIR / MICROCLIMATE

Guenoc Valley: soils vary; pockets of solidified magma high in magnesium.

VARIETALS GROWN

In Lake County: 74 acres Sauvignon Blanc, 111 Chardonnay, 44 Cabernet Sauvignon, 44 Petite Sirah, 3 Viognier, and 1 acre of Marsanne.

WINES PRODUCED

150,000 cases annually; 40% estate grown, 60% imported fruit.

WINE CLUB

Red, white, or mixed. 4 shipments per year. 20% off wines. Complimentary tasting for 4 at Estate. Members' newsletter.

Winemaking Philosophy

The 23,000-acre Langtry Estate is the largest contiguou landholding in California's premier North Coast AVA. With its volcanic past, the estate has a wide range of soils and microclimates. For Winemaker Walter Jorge, Langtry Estate is perfect for grapes. His goal is to produ wines that "express the characteristics of the vineyarc and terroir." He believes the wines are "full-bodied, rich and permeated with fragrance and fruit from this distinct site." The varied volcanic soils provide perfec growing conditions for a diverse range of varietals. Cabernet Sauvignon, Merlot and Petit Verdot enjoy the hillside slopes and mild summers, producing wines with soft phenolic tannin development and complexity Petite Sirah is planted in an area of solidified magma on the valley floor, which is restrictive in vigor, aiding intensity. Sauvignon Blanc and Chardonnay grapes favor the shallow clay loam on the Guenoc Valley floor which brings out the tropical fruit flavor in the wines.

Opposite: The lovely view from the picnic tables just outside the winery.

Below: Langtry as Cleopatra on the London stage; amazingly she gave 96 performances between 1890 and 1891. One of the most admired, photographed, and traveled women of her generation.

Lillie Langtry, a British-born stage actress and socialite, was one of the most celebrated women of her generation. Her famed acting career took her to America where she met wealthy romantic partner Freddie Gebhard. In 1888 they purchased adjoining land in the beautiful Guenoc Valley. Langtry started a successful wine operation (with her picture on the bottles). Gebhard ran a stud farm. With the help of a a French winemaker, she proceeded to produce what she declared to be " The finest Claret in America." The impressive long white picket fence, heralding her land, is an echo of the style and sophistication Lillie Langtry brought to the valley.

The modern winery built in 1981 resembles the old Langtry barn still standing across from the Gebhard Hunting Lodge two miles south. The winery over-looks the beautiful Detert Reservoir, where you may see Blue Heron, Snowy Egret, ducks, geese, and other waterfowl. Picnic tables are available to relax and enjoy the spectacular view with a glass of wine. Today the thriving modern winery has a wide variety of wines available to taste.

ADDRESS
21000 Butts Canyon Road
Middletown, CA 95461

CONTACT
707-995-7521
www.langtryestate.com
concierge@langtryestate.com

TASTING ROOM
Open Daily 10 am–5 pm.
$10 General tasting,
$15 Reserve tasting.
Langtry Estate Tour and Tasting $65,
($55 for club members).

FACILITIES
Spectacular picnic area overlooking lake, spacious gift shop, and popular guided tours.

EVENTS
Wine Adventure participant. See website and Facebook for more information.

WINERY HISTORY

David and Cheryl always enjoyed wine and dreamed of having a vineyard and small boutique winery. An opportunity to buy a 15-acre property in the Red Hills AVA was too good to miss. They planted their first vines in 2007 and opened a tasting room in 2013.

WINEMAKER BIO

Cheryl Lucido studied wine at UC Davis, obtaining a degree in Viticulture and Enology. She has been making wines since 2006, and from 2009, exclusively for Laujor.

ACREAGE / AVA

Total of 10 acres under vine, all within the Red Hills AVA.

ELEVATION

Highest about 2,400 feet.

TERROIR / MICROCLIMATE

Well-drained volcanic red soil, rich in minerals laced with obsidian.Typically a hot, dry growing season, lake influenced cooling breezes at night.

VARIETALS GROWN

4 acres of Cabernet Sauvignon, 4 Petite Sirah, 1 Syrah Noir, and 1 Cabernet Franc.

WINES PRODUCED

1,800 cases produced annually. 100% Lake County fruit. 80% from their estate: Cabernet Sauvignon, Petite Sirah, Syrah Noir, Cabernet Franc, Tempranillo, Rosé of Cabernet Franc. Wines from other Lake County fruit are: Sauvignon Blanc, Sangiovese, Malbec, and Zinfandel.

WINE CLUB

Memberships include the exclusive *Collector's Club* (1 case of ultra-premium wines semi-annually) to a *Reds of Distinction* red only club, and the *Portfolio Club* with mixed reds and whites. All clubs offer discounts, complimentary tastings for members' guests, invitations to private club events, and discounts for stays at the Laujor Vineyard Loft.

Winemaking Philosophy

The Lucidos both have a firm commitment to using farming practices that do not "compromise the future," and strive to create a vineyard management system that relies on prevention rather than cure. They take great care to cultivate healthy soils and carefully monitor the water and nutrients the vines receive. With these healthy soils they aim to "produce plants of good vigor, and the reduction of disease and pest incidence through proper water and nutrient management, results in improved yield and quality."

In terms of winemaking style, Cheryl likes to make "very approachable fruit forward full-bodied red wines," wine that is great to accompany a leisurely dinner–where it all began. The Lucidos' truly have one of the most spectacularly located wineries in the county. Laujor has become a popular destination to book for weddings and family parties.

Opposite: David and Cheryl Lucido on the spacious tasting room veranda with spectacular view of Mount Konocti.

Below: Cheryl, the winemaker, and guests examine the Cabernet.

D avid and Cheryl Lucido have always shared a passion for great wine and food. Like many, they often talked over dinner about perhaps owning a small production boutique winery one day.

When an opportunity to move to Lake County presented itself, they realized that dream could actually become a reality. They purchased a 15-acre parcel on a hillside in the acclaimed Red Hills AVA. The Lucidos set about clearing an overgrown walnut orchard which was on the site, and were overjoyed to reveal a spectacular vista of patchwork vineyards and sweeping views of Mt. Konocti.

The winery name "Laujor" may sound French, but it is actually a blend of the first three letters of their children Lauren and Jordan's names. Cheryl obtained a certificate in Viticulture and Enology at UC Davis in 2010. The Lucidos planted their first varietals on the site in 2007: Cabernet Sauvignon, Petite Sirah, Syrah Noir, and Cabernet Franc. Their estate Petite Sirah and Cabernet blends have taken gold more than once by a panel of professional judges.

ADDRESS
8664 Seigler Springs North Road
Kelseyville, CA 95451

CONTACT
707-349-8236
www.laujorestate.com
cheryl@laujorestate.com

TASTING ROOM
Open Daily 11 am–5 pm
Tasting is complimentary.

FACILITIES
Picnic area, vineyard tours, private tastings for groups of 6+.

EVENTS
Seasonal pick-up parties. Food and wine pairing events. Participant in Lake County Wine Adventure and the annual Barrels & Verticals Event. Accommodations are also available at the "Laujor Vineyard Loft." 707-349-4007 (for up to 4 people and pet-friendly with prior approval).

Winemaking Philosophy

The winemaker at Mt. Konocti Winery is Terry Goetze. Terry's winemaking history began in 2001 when his service in the U.S. Marine Corps ended. Being born in Michigan and raised in Napa piqued a natural interest for Terry in the wine industry. He has worked with a few ultra-premium wineries in Napa learning and perfecting his techniques working under the guidance of some of Napa's top winemakers. His career with Mt. Konocti began in the fall of 2015. Terry's philosophy is terroir driven– expression of the fruit and the soil it's grown in. He embraces unconventional winemaking techniques. Since coming on board Terry has brought the winery its first 90+ pt wines from the *Wine Enthusiast*.

Mt. Konocti Winery hosts the very popular Lake County "Wine and Chocolate" event in early Spring.

Opposite: The old packing shed-now a cool barrel and tasting room.

Below: Robert Gayaldo, the third generation of Gayaldos involved in the pear (and also now wine) industry in Lake County.

Mt. Konocti Winery

At the core of Lake County's agricultural history is the pear industry. The pear packing sheds in Big Valley were originally built in 1926 for the "Lake County Fruit Exchange." Established as a cooperatively owned facility for local pear farmers, it is still today actively engaged in the members' organic pear operations. It was re-named "Mt. Konocti Growers" in 1976, and at the height of pear production in the 1980s there were 68 growers. Today, with far fewer grower-members, the business has cleverly adapted with the times and is now one of the few wineries actually making wine on site. The winemaking plant was built in 2004, and many local wineries use their custom crush service.

Their own label, "Mt. Konocti Winery," wines were launched in 2007. They originally started making wine from the classic Lake County grape varietals: Cabernet Sauvignon, Sauvignon Blanc, and Zinfandel. They opened the tasting room in 2011, and today have expanded the wines they pour to include a Tempranillo, Zinfandel, Syrah, Viognier, Muscat, a Rosé, and a Late Harvest Sauvignon Blanc.

ADDRESS
2550 Big Valley Road,
Kelseyville, CA 95451
Mail: P.O. Box 365,
Kelseyville, CA 95451

CONTACT
707-279-4213
www.mtkonoctiwines.com
robert@mtkonoctiwines.com
info@mtkonoctiwines.com

TASTING ROOM
Open April-Oct., Sat-Sun, 12 pm–5 pm
Nov.-March, Sat only, 12 pm–5 pm
Tasting fee waived with purchase.

FACILITIES
Taste in the cool 58° F barrel room and tasting room. This large space is available to hire for many special occasions.

EVENTS
Hosts of the "Wine and Chocolate" event in early Spring each year. They are also participants in Lake County Wine Adventure.

Winemaking Philosophy

This small boutique operation is all about making fine handcrafted wines. Michael knows his terroir well and the effect it has on his grapes. In his first year at the site the daytime highs reached 117° F, so he set about changing the trellis system to better protect the grapes. He carefully monitors evapotranspiration rates on leaves and tastes the grapes to determine harvest time (not by using set brix or acidity levels). Yeast strains, barrel type, and toast level are also chosen based on that year's grape evaluation. The wines are unfiltered and unfined, giving a "chewy" viscosity that he feels holds the oak better. The rich deep color and full-bodied fruity quality are attributable to the high elevation and intense UV light in Lake County, producing small fruit with thick skins, where all the flavor and color come from. The style is very much his own, which he describes as "the best expression" of each unique vintage and flavor profile.

Opposite: Michael keeping track on the tractor at harvest time.

Noggle Vineyards & Winery 16

Michael Noggle planted his first vineyard back in 1977 and he has been a passionate home winemaker wherever his rich agricultural career has taken him. While he was living in St. Helena, in the Napa Valley, his wines began to receive considerable critical acclaim, so he decided to get serious and then obtained a degree in Viticulture and Enology from Napa College in the late 1990s.

Karen Noggle spotted the secluded Old Long Valley property for sale in the *San Francisco Chronicle* newspaper. Their visit to the beautiful vineyards turned a 30-year-long dream to make wine commercially into a reality. This is one of the first wineries in Lake County that visitors will pass traveling from the Sacramento area.

These high-elevation, well-draining volcanic soils "naturally stress the vines," perfect for the "nice, consumer-friendly, deep, rich, fruity, full-bodied Cabernets," he aims to make. Noggle also produces some Sauvignon Blanc from grapes grown in Finley, near the town of Kelseyville.

ADDRESS
700 Old Long Valley Road
Clearlake Oaks, CA 95423

CONTACT
707-998-0319
www.nogglevineyardsandwinery.com
nogglevineyard@aol.com

TASTING ROOM
By appointment only.
No tasting fee.

FACILITIES
Picnic area available. Guests are welcome to bring their own food, as no food available on site.

EVENTS
Participant in many Lake County wine seasonal events, such as Wine and Chocolate, Lake County Wine Adventure, and special events at The Lake County Wine Studio.

Winemaking Philosophy

Eric Olof, winemaker at Olof Cellars, has a playful and adventurous approach to winemaking. He likes to experiment by planting more unusual varietals, both to hone his craft and also to "separate us from the crowd." If Eric has a preference it is towards the "Cal-Ital" style of winemaking: "Great drinking wine that does not compete with any food." In this quest he favors more high-acidity grape varietals such as Barbera. He feels many varietals grown in Lake County require more acid to balance them, but in contrast Barbera "has to hang on the vine longer to lower the acid." No surprise as to why it is so popular in Italy; it pairs so beautifully with sausage, tomato, and cheese. The berry flavors and low tannins in the wine also make it an "easy drinker," a wine that is perfect to enjoy without food. The Malbec made by Olof Cellars is also a very popular wine.

Below: Olof Cellars converting rape and pillage to grape and tillage.

Owners Eric and Cindi Olof were originally from Aptos, though the name Olof comes from Eric's grandfather who emigrated to the Americas from Sweden. In their own way the Olofs are pioneers of their generation: they left sand and surf for wild and volcanic Lake County. The original intention was to farm and sell grapes, but then Eric, a self-taught winemaker, started making small batches of wine for himself. He found a keen demand for this wine and thus a small artisanal winery was born.

Olof is typical of a burgeoning number of small-scale boutique wineries gravitating to the county which employ a freer, more experimental approach to winemaking. They have chosen to plant some more unusual grape varieties; the red-fleshed "Lenoir" grape, for instance, is only grown by a handful of people in California.

They certainly make some very interesting wines, such as a single varietal Petit Verdot, a Barbera Rosé and a Sparkling Nebbiolo. These are wines you won't find everywhere–another rare Lake County gem.

ADDRESS
5615 Highlands Springs Road
Lakeport, CA 95453

CONTACT
707-391-7947
www.olofcellars.com
olofcellars@gmail.com

TASTING ROOM
Saturdays and holiday weekends.
11 am–5 pm. $5 tasting fee.
All other days by appointment.

FACILITIES
Picnic areas, dogs on leash welcome. Crafts in gift shop. ADA bathroom.

EVENTS
St. Olof's Day wine tour. Participant in Lake County Wine Adventure.

Winemaking Philosophy

The winemaker at Simi Winery in Sonoma County once suggested to Nick Buttitta that he should try making some of his own wine from the quality fruit he grew commercially. That idea lodged for many years. Nick was always experimenting with home winemaking, so when the time was right to start making his own wine he knew what he wanted to do. His dream was to produce quality wines from traditional Italian grape varietals. The wines, he says, are "crafted with a grower's eye, allowing the true personality of each varietal to shine through." The wines are all indeed handcrafted on site, mostly from estate fruit, but other varietals are also brought in to round out their impressive Italian wine collection. The Aglianico has received much critical acclaim. Rosa d'Oro is growing some rare Italian winegrapes: Negroamaro, Refosco, and Sagrantino. Why go to Italy when you have Rosa d'Oro in downtown Kelseyville!

Opposite: An offer you can't refuse, in fact, one you can bank on.
Below: "La Dolce Vita" vista. Olive & vine salute Mount Konocti.

The Buttitta family grew premium winegrapes in Santa Rosa from 1973 to 1983, supplying many of Sonoma's most prestigious wineries. In 1991 the family moved to Lake County and quickly recognized the quality of soils and climate. Nick wanted to try something different and honor his family roots by growing Italian varietals, grapes he thought could do well here. Nick's dream has been realized by the hard work of "La Famiglia."

Nick pulled from the four corners of his Italian heritage in selecting the grape varietals for his vineyards; he has planted Barbera and Dolcetto from the northwest, and Aglianico and Primitivo from the far southeast. He certainly knows his grapes *and* how to tame them for the Lake County climate.

There are other Italian touches, such as the planting of over 200 olive trees in and around the vineyards. The tasting room is housed in an historic bank in Kelseyville where they serve their olive oil alongside the impressive array of Italian-style wines.

ADDRESS
3915 Main Street
Kelseyville, CA 95451

CONTACT
707-279-0483
www.rosadorovineyards.com
info@rosadorovineyards.com

TASTING ROOM
Open Wed-Sat 11 am–6 pm
Sun 11 am–5 pm
Also open Mon-Tues 12 am–5 pm
from Memorial Day to Labor Day.
First five tastings complimentary.

FACILITIES
The tasting room is situated in the historic First Bank building in Kelseyville, built in 1910. The original bank vault houses a gift shop.

EVENTS
3 seasonal pick-up parties. Cannoli available the second Friday of each month. Participant in Wine Adventure.

Winemaking Philosophy

Joy Merrilees has a busy job as Director of Winemaking and Production at Shannon Ridge Family of Wines. That "family" is large and extended; there are special reserve single varietal wines of just a few hundred cases, some large-production branded wines, and some unique blends to be made each year. All have to be carefully tended and crafted. She is more than up to the job–as evidenced by the popularity of the wines she makes. A Lake County native, with a degree in Plant Science and Landscape Design from Humboldt State University, she worked for Steele Winery early on in her career. She honed her winemaking skills by travelling and working at wineries across the US, as well as spending many years winemaking and studying in New Zealand. Happily "back in her hometown" she is enjoying working with such "excellent fruit" and being a part of the rising acclaim for local wines.

Opposite: Sheep vigilantly weeding through their own tasting notes.
Below: The breathtaking view over Anderson Marsh.

Shannon Ridge Family of Wines 19

The former *Rolling Knolls* property (above) was well known to Clay Shannon as he had at one time managed the property. So little wonder he snapped up this most beautiful acreage when it became available. It has one of the most spectacular views in Lake County, looking across to Anderson Marsh, a large wetland preserve on a site with a long history. It has a prized northern aspect on the desirable rich volcanic soils of the Red Hills AVA.

This site has 5 steeply sloping knolls that lead down to the lake. The Shannon Ridge Family of Wines now has vineyards in five different AVAs in Lake County, all of which are sustainably farmed; the 1,000 head of sheep they use for weed control can often be seen grazing amongst the vines.

Many of the old farm buildings have been saved and re-purposed. The old farmhouse at Vigilance has a tasting room with stone cellar below. It is a really wonderful place to bring a picnic and sip a glass of the wine and drink in the breathtaking view. If you bring binoculars you might even spot a Bald Eagle.

ADDRESS
13888 Point Lakeview Road
Lower Lake, CA 95457

CONTACT
707-994-9656
www.shannonridge.com
info@shannonridge.com

TASTING ROOM (at Vigilance Vineyards)
Open Fri, Sat, Sun 11 am–5 pm
Open May-Dec. Closed in winter.

FACILITIES
Picnic area has beautiful views over Anderson Marsh wetlands, hiking trails, bocce ball court.

EVENTS
The Vigilance Tasting Room deck has lovely views over Anderson Marsh, and there is a great picnic area. There is a nice hiking trail between this property and the Gregory Graham Winery nearby. Participant in Lake County Wine Adventure.

OWNERS

Michael and Adawn Wood

WINERY HISTORY

The Shed Horn label was launched in 2004, with a 75-case initial production of a Cabernet Sauvignon. Today there are 6 varietals and a 4,500+ case production. The cozy tasting room opened in 2011.

WINEMAKER BIO

Michael Wood grew up in Lake County. He started his winemaking career back in 1982 at Guenoc Winery, where he learned on the job as winemaker of well-known California brands. He has also undertaken formal studies at Santa Rosa JC and UC Davis. His passionate and very hands-on approach for his craft have won him many prestigious awards.

ACREAGE / AVA

Grapes sourced from the Red Hills and High Valley AVAs, also from Long Valley, Clearlake Oaks and Kelsey Bench.

ELEVATION

Various, all over 2,000 feet.

TERROIR / MICROCLIMATE

As typifies each AVA listed.

VARIETALS

Chardonnay, Cabernet Sauvignon, Petite Sirah, Sauvignon Blanc, Zinfandel, and some Barbera, Grenache, Petit Verdot and Syrah, all locally sourced.

WINES PRODUCED

4,500+ cases produced annually. All 100% from Lake County fruit, mostly single varietal wines: Chardonnay, Sauvignon Blanc, Cabernet Sauvignon, Petite Sirah, Zinfandel and a Grenache Rosé. Their award winning blend "Non Typical Red Wine" is a blend of Zinfandel, Syrah, Cabernet Sauvignon, Barbera, Petit Verdot and Petite Sirah.

WINE CLUB

Wine club offers different levels of membership from 6-12 bottles annually. 20% discount on sales. $1 wine by the glass, complimentary tasting, and invites to release parties.

Winemaking Philosophy

Michael Wood has been making wine in Lake County for over 30 years, so he knows this diverse landscape with its multiple "terroirs" very well. His winemaking philosophy is very much one of sourcing the very best grapes and not getting in their way too much while they are busy making wine. He is in a great position to acquire great locally grown fruit, and then knows what to do (or not) with it. He began in 2004 with a small 3-barrel lot of Cabernet Sauvignon and made 75 cases. His 2006 vintage Cabernet won a Double Gold and Best of Class at the *San Francisco Chronicle Wine Competition*. In fewer than a dozen years Shed Horn Cellars has now expanded to 4,500+ cases and has opened a small intimate tasting room in downtown Middletown. Though the production is increasing, this family-run winery still wants to retain the hand-crafted, small lot artisanal feel to both its wines and its business.

Opposite: Vines on a sunny hillside in the Cross Springs Vineyard in Clearlake Oaks, getting ready to shed those grapes.

Below: Adawn offers some typical, and some not-so-typical, Shed Horn wines to guests in her cozy tasting room in uptown/downtown Middletown.

Shed Horn Cellars 20

Michael Wood was born in Petaluma but has spent most of his formative years in Lake County. He met his high school sweetheart–now wife–Adawn in Middletown, and together they are developing a strong and respected brand in this small boutique winery. The name Shed Horn is a nod to Michael's love of the outdoors. He once found a large elk's shed horn on a hunting trip. His dad was a bronc rider and Michael and his 3 brothers thrived in this wild open country. His passion for wine is also focused outside–in the vineyard–and on the key decisions he makes there.

Michael learned his craft locally at Guenoc Winery, which he joined in 1982. He worked for many other wineries in the area, repeatedly gaining valuable experience. His great knowledge and passion for wine has won him many awards.

Both are justly proud of the many accolades they have been getting in and out of state. Production, however, is small, and most of this wine doesn't leave the county–another great reason to visit.

ADDRESS
21108 Calistoga Road, #4,
Middletown, CA 95461

CONTACT
Tasting room: **707-987-8445**
Mobile: **707-291-3629**
www.shedhorncellars.com
adawn@shedhorncellars.com

TASTING ROOM
Fri-Sat noon-6pm Jan-Feb.
Thur-Sun noon-6pm March-Dec.
Special appointments welcome.
$5 tasting fee, complimentary to
wine club members.

FACILITIES
Wine bar, local gifts, food available.

EVENTS
Pick-up parties April and October.
Holiday season specials and new
release special events.

OWNERS

Kaj and Else Ahlmann

WINERY HISTORY

The Asbill Valley Ranch was first settled in 1859. This historic ranch and adjacent parcels now form the 4,300 acres the Ahlmanns bought in 2000. At the newly named "Six Sigma Ranch" they found evidence of many old pioneer families who first settled the area. Else has researched and written a fascinating book about the ranch history. The first vineyard was planted in 2001 and the winery and cave were completed in 2005.

WINEMAKER BIO

Sandy Robertson was educated at Plumpton College, a specialist land-based college in the UK. He then worked at wineries in France and England. He was the assistant wine-maker at Merry Edwards Winery in Sonoma, before joining Six Sigma.

ACREAGE / AVA

Total of 40 acres under vine in the Lake County appellation.

ELEVATION

Between 1,300–2,200 feet.

TERROIR / MICROCLIMATE

The large 4,300-acre Six Sigma Ranch has a wide range of different soil types and microclimates.

VARIETALS GROWN

12 acres of Sauvignon Blanc, 2 Pinot Noir, 2 Syrah, 1 Petit Verdot, 2 Merlot, 14 Cabernet Sauvignon, and 7 Tempranillo.

WINES PRODUCED

9,000 cases produced annually. 100% estate grown; mostly the single varietals listed above plus a popular Rosé and *Diamond Cuvée*, a blend of Cabernet Sauvignon, Tempranillo, and Syrah.

WINE CLUB

Wine club offers different types of membership; 3 bottles quarterly; mixed, red or white only. 20% discount on all wines. Many excellent special events (see website).

Winemaking Philosophy

The Ahlmann family is committed to creating a healthy ecosystem on the ranch, enabling the fruit to reach peak condition. This goal fits perfectly with Sandy Robertson's winemaking philosophy: "to simplify wherever possible, to minimize inputs, additions and manipulations by starting with the best possible fruit and paying attention to details." The combined efforts have resulted in award-winning wines. The key to the *Six Sigma* methodology is to carefully gather and analyze data, aiming at consistently high quality. Examples of the steps they use to monitor the grape growing and winemaking are: choice of root stock; canopy management; pest control (using beneficial insects); harvesting times; and fermentation temperatures. With degrees in Viticulture and Oenology, Sandy Robertson is well prepared to assess every step in the process. In the vineyard he is working closely with Christian, the oldest Ahlmann son. All of this careful attention to detail certainly shows in their wines.

Opposite: A new day dawns over the 4,300-acre Six Sigma Ranch.
Below: Even the sheep have embraced the biodiversity mission.

Six Sigma Ranch & Winery

Kaj and Else Ahlmann met in 1966 in Denmark where they were born and raised; they both loved nature from an early age. Kaj helped grow crops on his family's farm in Denmark when he was just 14 years old, learning organic farming and conservation principles from his grandpa.

In 1993 Kaj's work led to a relocation in Kansas, and the family and four children settled there for many years. In 2000 the Ahlmanns bought the 4,300-acre ranch near Lower Lake. This was the end of a long search for the perfect location to realize a life-long dream to start a farm/winery.

Strictly sustainable farming practices are used on the ranch. Sheep roam throughout the vines for weed control; a herd of grass-fed cattle graze in the pasturelands. Harmful pesticides are rejected in favor of beneficial insect programs. True to their belief of being the "stewards" of this amazingly beautiful property, they have placed a conservation easement on it to protect it and the amazing variety of wildlife that live there, for posterity.

ADDRESS
13372 Spruce Grove Road
Lower Lake, CA 95457

CONTACT
707-994-4068 or **888-571-1721**
www.sixsigmaranch.com
communicate@sixsigmaranch.com

TASTING ROOM (2 miles from gate)
Open Daily 11 am–4:30 pm
$10 tasting fee for current releases.
Vineyard tours in an all-terrain
Pinzgauer, Saturdays at 10 am, noon,
and 2 pm; $20/person, private tours
available, minimum 6 people.

FACILITIES
Picnic area, hiking trail, pizza oven
for special occasions.

EVENTS
Ranch to Table dinners in summer,
"Flight Night" in October, International
"Tempranillo Day in November.
Participant in Wine Adventure.

OWNER

Scott Simkover

WINERY HISTORY

The first vintage was released from the winery in 2008. Their own vineyard was planted in 2013.

WINEMAKER BIO

Scott Simkover is largely self taught in the artisanal tradition, but has also consulted with many of Lake County's most established winemakers.

ACREAGE / AVA

The 2 estate acres are in the Kelsey Bench AVA. Other grapes are all sourced from Lake County AVAs, and all are organically grown.

ELEVATION

Average 1,300 feet on ranch.

TERROIR / MICROCLIMATE

Well drained, deep, gravelly, and volcanic soils of Kelsey Bench.

VARIETALS GROWN

1¾ acre of Zinfandel and a ¼ acre of Barbera are grown on the ranch. Other varietals are all produced from Lake County fruit, most sourced within 5 miles of the winery.

WINES PRODUCED

800-1,400 cases produced annually. Estate grown and bottled wines are currently 30% of total and rising. Single varietal wines produced: Tempranillo, Cabernet Sauvignon, Sauvignon Blanc and Merlot. Blends produced: 'Sophie's Choice' (Merlot and Zinfandel), 'SyrahZinLot' (Syrah, Zinfandel and Merlot), 'Fusion'(50/50 Cabernet and Merlot), 'BraZen' (Barbera and Zinfandel). The latter is an estate blend.

WINE CLUB

Wine club offers members 6 bottles per year for $125. Members can choose any combination of red, white or blends. Members enjoy complimentary tastings and 20% discount on all wine purchases.

Winemaking Philosophy

Although there's plenty of science in winemaking, and it's his background, Scott Simkover is firmly of the opinion that winemaking is an Art too. This philosophy is in accord with small artisanal wine producers the world over. These winemakers are super-hands-on, producing small batch wines which they personally oversee "from grape to glass" as he says. His goal is to make high-quality small batch wines "accessible."

His mission is also to use very ecologically-friendly farming methods. The winery is powered with renewable energy from sun & wind. He grows his fruit according to strict sustainable farming practices and sources grapes from others who farm the same way. Ten years on he has created a wide variety of wines and wine styles, with some very interesting blends. The tasting room offers a large selection of his well-regarded wines open and ready to taste.

Opposite: Scott with his two smiling assistants, Sophie and Vino.
Below: The friendly tasting room is one of five within walking distance.

Smiling Dogs Ranch 22

Scott Simkover moved to the San Francisco Bay Area in the 60s to study Biology and Medical Technology. A career as a clinical lab scientist ensued which led him to Oregon, where the craft beer movement was taking off. He became a passionate small batch brewer, nearly accepting an invitation to pursue that professionally. It was not until he came to St. Helena Hospital Clearlake in 2006, as a travelling lab scientist, that his fermenting skills turned towards wine.

The appeal of a small agricultural community, and a chance to make wine all felt right, so he bought a 5-acre ranch and began his vineyard. Some local winemakers were very generous with advice, and he soon had a fully equipped winery, fuelled by renewable energy. The name Smiling Dogs Ranch is the result of a competition he held, which was won by a friend who knew his love of Samoyed dogs–a breed he's had for years. The dogs, from Siberia, are used to keep people warm and happy...funny, the wines do that too!

ADDRESS
Tasting room: 3955 Main Street
Kelseyville, CA 95451
Winery: 6675 Kelsey Creek Drive
Kelseyville, CA 95451

CONTACT
707-279-2762
www.smilingdogsranch.com
apocalypsewines@gmail.com

TASTING ROOM
Open Fri 2 pm–5 pm, Sat 11 am–7 pm,
Sun 12 am–5 pm. Tasting fee of $5 is
waived with bottle purchase.

FACILITIES
Tasting room displays local artists'
work and has space for bands.

EVENTS
Futures release party in February,
plus 5-6 wine club parties over the
summer. Live music each Friday night
in tasting room. Participant in Lake
County Wine Adventure.

OWNERS
Bryan Kane and Jill Brothers

WINERY HISTORY
The Lake County winery started in 2005 with the purchase of the 70-acre parcel of land in the Red Hills area. At the start they used some out-of-county fruit, but by 2008 most of the wines were made from Lake County fruit. In 2012 they opened a tasting room in San Francisco.

WINEMAKER BIO
Bryan left Michigan for business school in California. A long-time passion for fine wines soon led to a more active involvement in the thriving wine industry he discovered out west. He apprenticed with many notable winemakers in Napa and Sonoma, gaining valuable hands-on experience before starting his own Sol Rouge label in 2005.

ACREAGE / AVA
Total of 6 acres under vine within the Red Hills AVA.

ELEVATION
Average about 1,800 feet.

TERROIR / MICROCLIMATE
Well-drained, rocky volcanic red soil rich in minerals; steeply sloping hillsides, many different aspects on site. Typically hot summer days with cool breezes from the lake.

VARIETALS GROWN
1 acre Grenache, 1 Cabernet Sauvignon, plus .5 acre or less of Syrah, Zinfandel, Mourvèdre, Petite Sirah, Counoise, Cinsault, and Cabernet Franc.

WINES PRODUCED
1,200 cases produced annually. 90% of wines from Lake County fruit. Many single varietals as listed above, but also some interesting blends.

WINE CLUB
Wine club offers two levels of membership, 6 or 12 bottles twice a year. A 15% and 25% discount, respectively.

Winemaking Philosophy

The 70 acres Bryan Kane bought in the Red Hills AVA has varied and interesting topography. He says it has "just about every aspect but due east." It has very steep slopes, as much as 50° in some areas, and also pockets where the surrounding mountains and hillsides offer some shade and protection from the hottest days. This gives him a "lot to play with" in terms of the selection of grape varietals that can thrive here, and he'd like to try some more. Bryan's philosophy is very much that "wine is made in the field," and that a "non-intervention" policy is one that brings the true flavor and characteristics of the vineyard through to the wines. He is deeply involved in all aspects of viticulture as well as the winemaking, and does not use chemicals or add artificial yeast to his wines. He wants to taste the unique flavors that come from the red soil. These methods are bearing fruit–he recently celebrated a 90+ point rating by *Wine Enthusiast* magazine for each of his 9 recently released wines.

Opposite: View of the McKinney Block of the vineyard (named after the previous landowners) on a steep western-facing slope.

Below: Terrace Block with slopes over 50°. Sol, Soleil, et Voila!

S ol Rouge, a French name, translates to "red soil," and the soils of the very desirable Red Hills AVA are indeed red *and* hilly. Many recognizable "Napa names" have been staking claim to their own little (and not so little) slices of this red-hot terroir for a while now. The giant Beckstoffer vineyards are now their next door neighbor. When Bryan Kane and Jill Brothers bought the 70 acres back in 2005, "there were just 10 or 11 wineries in Lake County," he says. Sol Rouge was one of the original members of the Lake County Winery Association.

Like many farming the Red Hills, Bryan recognized the similarity of this area's terroir to that of Bordeaux and the Southern Rhône, two world-class French wine regions. Bryan set about planting many classic French varietals, not just Cabernet and Grenache, but also some less well known grape varietals, such as Counoise, Cinsault, and Cabernet Franc. The experiment has paid off–his first release of Cabernet Franc was named "Top Cabernet Franc in America" by the *S.F. Chronicle* Wine Competition, and many more accolades have been pouring in.

ADDRESS
5395 Konocti Road,
Kelseyville, CA 95451
29 Avenue G,
San Francisco, CA 94130

CONTACT
415-756-2254 or **707-279-9000**
www.solrouge.com
info@solrouge.com

TASTING ROOM
Lake County: Open by appointment at vineyard site, no tasting fee.
And San Francisco:
Open Sat-Sun 12–5 pm
Tasting fee $15 for 6 pours.

FACILITIES
Picnic areas at Lake County and San Francisco sites. SF has a waterfront location with a BBQ and bocce ball courts.

EVENTS
Seasonal pick-up parties.

OWNER
Jed Steele

WINERY HISTORY
Jed started his own winery in 1991 after making wine for prestigious wineries in Napa and Mendocino.

WINEMAKER BIO
Jed has 50 years in the business and enjoys making a wide variety of wine from a very broad spectrum of grape varietals. Quincy, Jed's son, focuses on more locally grown varietals.

ACREAGE / AVA
40 acres total under vine in Kelsey Bench and Big Valley AVAs.

ELEVATION
Average about 1,450 feet.

TERROIR / MICROCLIMATE
3 different sites in Lake County.

VARIETALS GROWN
13.5 acres of Merlot, 7.3 Zinfandel, 6.4 Syrah, 7 Cabernet Franc, 1 Counoise, 2 Petit Verdot, 2 Malbec, and 0.6 Tempranillo.

WINES PRODUCED
70,000 cases produced annually. 52% of the fruit is grown in Lake County: Sauvignon Blanc, Syrah, Counoise, Zinfandel, Cabernet Franc, and Merlot. From Washington State: Aligote and Blaufrankisch. Sonoma: Chardonnay, Pinot Noir, and Syrah. Santa Barbara: Chardonnay, Pinot Blanc, and Pinot Noir. Mendocino: Chardonnay and Zinfandel. The *Steele* label, the largest, has wines that can be aged. The *Shooting Star* wines are lighter, brighter, designed to be enjoyed young. *Writer's Block* focuses on locally sourced fruit. *Stymie* is the *Founder's Reserve* Merlot and Syrah.

WINE CLUB
Ships to members 4 times a year. Premium, reds, or mixed. A 20% discount on all wines and 10% on gift shop items. Spring and Holiday Club Members party.

Winemaking Philosophy

Jed's early career in Napa and Mendocino gave him the broad experience and valuable opportunity to "produce wines from just about every top quality wine region in the state, from Santa Barbara to Mendocino." When Jed decided to start his own winery in Lake County 23 years later, he did so "to once again be in very close contact with the vineyards and wines that I was making, something that had gotten lost for me in the world of large corporate wineries." He says he takes an "informed, minimalistic approach to the crafting of the wines," such as using natural yeast, avoiding any extra additives or enzymes, and using gravity flow to move wines to avoid "bruising" them. He thinks a "lighter hand" will "highlight the aromas and flavors of the quality fruit we source." He loves to experiment with more obscure, esoteric varietals such as Aligote and Blaufrankisch. Son Quincy has his own *Writer's Block* label, which also features some unusual grape varieties, such as Counoise.

Opposite: Red wines are aged in French, Hungarian, and American oak barrels. Below: The whites go into large stainless tanks.

Jed's family left New York for San Francisco in the 1940s thanks to a winning bet his father made on a race horse named *Stymie*. Jed was later to name his premium "Founders Reserve" Merlot and Syrah wines after this auspicious start.

Jed started in California's wine industry in 1968 as a cellar worker at Stony Hill in Napa. He obtained his Master's degree in Enology from UC Davis. He then was a key player in the startup of two very successful wineries; Edmeades in the Anderson Valley and Kendall-Jackson in Lake County. These experiences led to a well-respected reputation in the industry, and perhaps inevitably into starting his own winery, which he did in 1991.

With a great appreciation for many different grape varietals and wine styles, Jed has created one of the most diverse collections of interesting and high quality wines in the county. The sheer range of wines on display in the tasting room might lead one to believe this is a massive operation–but in actual fact many of these wines are crafted in quite small lots.

ADDRESS
4350 Thomas Drive,
Kelseyville, CA 95451

CONTACT
707-279-9475 or 888-533-7946
www.steelewines.com

TASTING ROOM
Open Mon-Sat 11 am–5 pm
From May to October open Sat 8:30 am–5 pm to coincide with the early morning summer Farmers Market held on Sat 8:30 am–12 pm.
$5 tasting fee.

FACILITIES
Large picnic area in front of the winery, gift items for sale.

EVENTS
Farmers Market May to Oct, Sat. 8:30 am–12 pm. Pick-up parties twice a year. A popular Harvest Festival event is held on the 2nd weekend in Oct. Participant in Wine Adventure.

Winemaking Philosophy

Friends, Greg Stratmann and Clinton Jones have a wealth of combined scientific knowledge to draw on when hand-crafting the wines for Stonehouse Cellars. Both would also acknowledge, however, that quality winemaking is as much about the art of farming as it is science. The vineyard sits on a shelf above Cache Creek, at elevations ranging between 1,400-1,500 ft., high enough to enjoy the strong UV light which adds intense flavor to the grapes, and low enough to catch the cool breezes from nearby High Valley. The site also, fortunately, has some very different soil types including a white tufa (found in the classic white wine regions of France and Italy), and some red volcanic soils, which Lake County red wines are now famous for. They also strive to keep fruit production per vine low so that "each grape is more flavorful." Their goal to produce small-lot, ultra-premium, estate wines "layered with complexity" is certainly barreling along.

Below: The historic "Pomo Statue" sits next to vines on the ranch.

OWNERS
Greg Stratmann and Jimee Hwang

WINERY HISTORY
Greg Stratmann and Clinton Jones first purchased the vineyard in 2010, revitalized the vines and then collected their first harvest in 2013. The first bottling of an estate-grown Cabernet was in 2017. The winery construction was also completed that year.

WINEMAKER BIO
Clinton Jones was originally from farming stock in Kansas before embarking on a career as a medical scientist. He has a certificate in winemaking from UC Davis and is also very involved in the Viticulture at Stonehouse Cellars.

ACREAGE / AVA
Total of 16.5 acres under vine.

ELEVATION
Between 1,400–1,500 feet.

TERROIR / MICROCLIMATE
Varied: notably some very well-drained, volcanic red soil rich in minerals, and some blocks with white tufa. Typically hot, dry summers with cool breezes in late afternoon.

VARIETALS GROWN
90% Cabernet Sauvignon,
10% Sauvignon Blanc and Viognier.

WINES PRODUCED
1,000 cases produced annually.
90% from estate fruit.
Estate wines: Cabernet Sauvignon, Voignier, and Sauvignon Blanc.
Also from Lake County fruit: a dry-farmed Red Hills AVA Merlot, and a Grenache and a Grenache Rosé.
Wines from other AVAs: Pinot Noir, Zinfandel.

WINE CLUB
Different levels of memberships and case commitments. 20% discount on wine purchases and winery accommodations. Complimentary tastings and invites to club events.

Stonehouse Cellars

25

Choosing the name "Bed & Barrel" to describe the elegant hospitality offered at this beautiful new winery reflects the "lack of pomp and circumstance" that attracted the owners to Lake County's wine region in the first place.

Stonehouse Cellars was started by three scientist friends, from Silicon Valley, with a passion for winemaking. These two families were also seeking a place to escape from city life, a haven, to relax, recharge and rediscover the "small and simple miracles" of daily life which are so easy to lose sight of in all the "hustle and bustle."

When the historic Pomo Ranch and vineyard in Lake County became available, Greg Stratmann, wife Jimee Hwang, and fellow scientist and winemaking friend, Clinton Jones decided to set about realizing this dream. The Stratmanns choose Matt Hollis to design the winery, which is perfectly sited to enjoy the breathtaking views. This impressive, yet warm, building is set to become a cherished sanctuary for lucky guests.

ADDRESS
500 Old Long Valley Road
Clearlake Oaks, CA 95423

CONTACT
707-998-3378
www.stonehousecellars.com
info@stonehousecellars.com
bedandbarrel@stonehousecellars.com

TASTING ROOM
By appointment only.
$25 tasting and touring fee
$45 lunch with tasting & touring.
$65 expanded lunch with tasting & touring.

FACILITIES
Picnic area, vineyard tours, Agricultural Homestay and Bed & Breakfast.

EVENTS
Seasonal release parties. Food and wine pairing classes. Available for private events. Participant in Lake County Wine Adventure.

OWNERS

Jack and Amy Thorn

WINERY HISTORY

The Thorns bought the 50-acre parcel in the Red Hills AVA in 2005. In 2007 they produced their first Lake County wine, their *Volcanic Rock Reserve* Cabernet Sauvignon from 100% Red Hills Cabernet grapes. In 2012 they opened their tasting room.

WINEMAKER BIO

Amy Thorn, the winemaker, developed a love of wine while studying abroad at college. After graduating she studied winemaking at UC Davis and traveled to the world's best wine growing regions to further enhance her skills as a winemaker. She is also a professional wine judge.

ACREAGE / AVA

Total of 50 acres in the Red Hills AVA.

ELEVATION

Average 2,000 feet.

TERROIR / MICROCLIMATE

Well-drained, red volcanic soil with obsidian rocks. 50˚F diurnal temperature changes are possible.

VARIETALS GROWN

Cabernet Sauvignon

WINES PRODUCED

3,500 cases produced annually. 100% sustainably farmed grapes. Wines from Lake County grapes: *Volcanic Rock Reserve* Cabernet Sauvignon, Petite Sirah Port, Petite Sirah, Old Vine Zinfandel, Pinot Grigio, and Sauvignon Blanc. From Napa: Chardonnay, late-harvest Sauvignon Blanc-Semillion, Cabernet Sauvignon, Merlot and Petite Sirah. From Sonoma: Pinot Noir and Merlot. From the North Coast: Riesling and *Brut de Prestige* Sparkling Wine.

WINE CLUB

Club membership gives access to limited release wines at a discount and invitations to a wide variety of popular winery events.

Winemaking Philosophy

Amy Thorn, owner and winemaker of Thorn Hill Vineyards, is one of an innovative group of new Californian women winemakers. Her unique style "balances intellect with intuition." She is committed to quality with a guiding principle that all of her wines reflect their distinctive terroir and embody the hallmark characteristics of each varietal. Every wine is 100% varietal-pure and is bottled unfined and unfiltered. She believes that making great wine is a "balance of experience, intuition, discipline and discovery." Each vintage is crafted by premium fruit selection, meticulous winemaking and master blending. There are now 16 limited production, artisan wines. Amy believes the greatest gift she can give as a winemaker is to "create a bottle of wine that is the purest expression of each varietal, a wine that is a combination of nature and nurture, and represents a union between fruit of the vine, the richness of the earth and the passion of the winemaker."

Below: The elegant Red Hills tasting room is a cool spot to escape the heat. The three luxurious Vineyard Villa Suites on the property are the perfect place to stay, taste the full range of wines, and explore the wine country.

At the turn of the millennium—with passion, a dream and 20 years of studying, exploring and appreciating fine wines—Amy Thorn took a leap of faith: together with her husband Jack, she founded Thorn Hill Vineyards. The mineral-rich volcanic soils in the Red Hills Appellation of Lake County proved to be ideally suited for the single varietal fine wines that are a hallmark of Thorn Hill.

Thorn Hill Vineyards is a family enterprise, with all Amy and Jack's adult children actively involved in its operations. Amy personally supervises every aspect of the wine production: the hand-harvesting, crushing, fermentation, barreling, blending, and aging in French oak barrels. Jack's background in biology and botany is applied to the vineyards. Son Jonathan oversees the production, tasting room and bed-and-breakfast Villa Suites. Daughter Rachael manages their historic Pennsylvania tasting room. The casual elegance of the lovely Lake County Tasting Room is the perfect setting to discover Thorn Hill's handcrafted, small lot, single varietal wines.

ADDRESS
8170 South Highway 29
Lower Lake, CA 95457

CONTACT
707-279-2745
www.thornhillvineyards.com
info@ThornHillVineyards.com

TASTING ROOM
Open Daily 11 am–5 pm
$5 tasting fee waived with purchase.

FACILITIES
Luxury bed and breakfast Vineyard Villa Suites, private weddings and receptions. Palazzo patios with fountain/fireplaces and panoramic vineyard views.

EVENTS
"Magical Musical Nights", wine and food pairings, club parties, winemaker dinners. Participant in Lake County Wine Adventure. See website for details.

WINERY HISTORY
Wildhurst was founded by Myron and Marilyn Holdenried. Holdenried was one of the "old" pioneer families of Lake County. Myron was one of the first in the county to grow grapes, and in 1966 he planted 30 acres of Zinfandel grapes. Michael and Tanya acquired the property in 2017. Michael's family also have a long history of winegrape growing.

WINEMAKER BIO
Stephen Dilley joined the Wildhurst team in July 2015 and was the winemaker of record for the 2015 vintage. He has a Certificate of Special Study in Enology, a post-baccalaureate degree in winemaking from Fresno State University.

ACREAGE / AVA
150 acres under vine, 130 on "Home Ranch" in the new Big Valley AVA, and 20 within the Kelsey Bench AVA.

ELEVATION
Between 1,400-1,450 feet.

TERROIR / MICROCLIMATE
Home Ranch: gravelly clay loam soils, warm days, cool evening breezes from the lake. 20 acres of Cabernet on the north slopes of Kelsey Bench on red Aiken clay loam soils.

VARIETALS GROWN
21 acres of Sauvignon Blanc, 16 Riesling, 10 Chardonnay, 6 Muscat, 10 Zinfandel, 10 Syrah, 30 Merlot, and 20 Cabernet Sauvignon.

WINES PRODUCED
12,000 cases produced annually. 95% wines are from Lake County fruit, mostly single varietal wines.

WINE CLUB
Offers members 2-3 bottles per quarter. A 25% discount on all wines and 50% discount on cases. There is also a 10% discount on tasting room merchandise. Member case sales.

Winemaking Philosophy

The winery, built in 1997, is situated next to the former Holdenried pear packing shed. It is equipped with state-of-the-art technology and has a 70,000 case capacity annually. Winemaker Stephen Dilley studied winemaking at Fresno State University obtaining a Certificate of Special Study in Enology, a post-baccalaureate degree in winemaking. Stephen then moved to Nice, California where he has worked in local wineries and also commuted to wineries in Napa and Sonoma Counties. Stephen joined the Wildhurst team in July 2015. In addition to his work at Wildhurst, Stephen also consults as winemaker for a few small winemaking concerns. Stephen's wines have won numerous awards and he has received many accolades from the public and peers alike.

Opposite: Home Ranch during harvest time.

Below: The Wildhurst tasting room in the characterful "Odd Fellows Hall." The odd, and the not so odd, all happily blend together at this lively spot.

Wildhurst Vineyards

27

M yron Holdenried, the founder of Wildhurst, is a member of one of the first European families to settle in Lake County back in 1856. Those original farmers grew all kinds of fruit, including grapes, but post-Prohibition the area turned its attention to pears.

Myron's great grandfather, Lewis Henderson, was one of the first to start commercial pear farming in the county. The decline in that industry in the 1950s caused forward-looking farmers to diversify into other crops. In the 1860s Lake County had been a thriving grape growing area; Myron decided to re-visit this.

In 1966 Myron planted his first 30 acres, on former cattle pasture land. He chose to plant Zinfandel grapes, a varietal California was very well known for. The Holdenrieds' success at growing winegrapes led them to construct a fully-equipped winery in a former pear shed, and build a successful wine brand with a tasting room in Kelseyville. The new owners, Michael and Tanya Hat, are proud and excited to be continuing the Holdenreids' love of farming and winemaking excellence. Michael Hat is a third-generation grower of winegrapes from the Central Valley.

ADDRESS
Tasting room: 3855 Main Street, Kelseyville, CA 95451
Mail: PO Box 1310 Kelseyville, CA 95451

CONTACT
707-279-4302 or 800-595-9463
www.wildhurst.com
info@wildhurst.com

TASTING ROOM
Open Daily 11 am–5 pm
No tasting fee for 5 pours.
Closed for major holidays.

FACILITIES
Courtyard with clay oven, picnic area. Spacious tasting room sells wide variety of local foods and crafts, as well as many wine-related gifts.

EVENTS
Club release parties and winemaker dinners. A Harvest Gathering in Fall. Participant in Lake County Wine Adventure. See website.

LCWS Wine Selection

The Lake County Wine Studio was first established in 2007 by Matt Hughes (now winemaker at Brassfield) and two other business partners. In those early days they offered tastings for a group of just 6 local wineries. When Susan Feiler, a native from the San Francisco Bay Area, moved to the county she originally joined the studio as an employee. Impressed by the quality and variety of wine she found in Lake County, she was also quick to identify that many other small, more artisanal producers also needed to showcase their wines some-where. In 2008 she took over the Studio and expanded the wines she represents to the current impressive selection. While the Studio focuses on the smaller producer, Susan also rounds out her collection with some wines from the larger wineries, the goal being to provide as broad a spectrum of quality wines produced in the county as possible in one location.

The Wine Club

The studio has a very active and well-supported wine club, offering members all kinds of discounts on wines, invitations to events such as wine and food pairings, gallery opening nights, and private wine tours.

Below: An Obsidian Ridge food and wine pairing event is enjoyed by locals.

WINES POURED*

ALIÉNOR
BEAVER CREEK
BIG VALLEY
BOATIQUE WINERY
BODKIN
BRASSFIELD ESTATE
BULLION ROUGE
CACHE CREEK
CHACEWATER
COUGAR'S LEAP
DANCING CROW VINEYARDS
DON ANGEL CELLARS
FORE FAMILY
FULTS FAMILY VINEYARDS
GREGORY GRAHAM
HAGAFEN CELLARS
HAWK & HORSE
KAZ / LAKEPORT WINERY
LADY OF THE LAKE
LANGTRY
LAUJOR ESTATE
MOORE FAMILY WINERY
MT. KONOCTI WINERY
NOGGLE VINEYARDS & WINERY
OBSIDIAN RIDGE
OLOF CELLARS
R VINEYARDS
RED LAVA
ROBLEDO FAMILY
ROSA D'ORO
SHANNON RIDGE FAMILY OF WINES
SHED HORN CELLARS
SIX SIGMA
SMILING DOGS
SOL ROUGE
STEELE WINES
STONEHOUSE CELLARS
TEJADA
THORN HIILL
TWO ANGELS
WILDHURST VINEYARDS

*Subject to availability

Lake County Wine Studio

28

Located in the historic town of Upper Lake, the Lake County Wine Studio (LCWS) is a must-visit destination for the adventurous wine tourist. The studio is located in a spacious building with a long curving tasting bar and a cozy fireside seating area. The space doubles as an art gallery that showcases local artists and craft workers on a rotating basis.

An impressive 190 local wines are available for sale, and a surprisingly large number of these are made available to taste on any given day. It is the perfect place to sample the sheer diversity (and quality) of varietals grown in Lake County. Many of the smaller, artisanal, family wineries often do not yet have tasting rooms of their own, and so the LCWS gives these often small production wines the chance to be poured. All the wines represented are either made in Lake County or are made from local winegrapes at custom crush facilities in or out of the county. They hold many fun events such as wine & art classes and regular food & wine pairings evenings.

ADDRESS
9505 Main Street, PO Box 104
Upper Lake, CA 95485

CONTACT
707-275-8030
susan@lakecountywinestudio.com

TASTING ROOM
Open Thur-Mon 1 pm–7 pm,
Fri 1 pm–8 pm
Six pour tasting $8.

EVENTS
A food and wine pairing event is held the first Friday of each month in which a flight of a local winery's wines is paired with a guest chef's food suggestions. Each month the gallery has an opening night for a featured local artist or craft person. The Studio also arranges some private winery tours.

Boutique Wines of Lake County

Where to find Boutique Wines

While wine touring in Lake County, it might be easy to miss some of the outstanding smaller-lot, artisanal wines being produced if it were not for Susan Feiler's Lake County Wine Studio in Upper Lake. Luckily for the wine enthusiast, Susan has adeptly sought out many of the very best smaller boutique winemakers (who don't have tasting rooms or a big retail presence), and has assembled them all into one place– much like a quality wine merchant in Europe would. Lake County is a fascinating area for the wine-lover because the *whole gamut* is here; there are self-taught winemakers making award-winning wines in their barns, there are notable winemakers who want to make smaller-lot wines from unusual varietals they have brought from their homelands, and there are some pretty big-dog, best-in-show winemakers who are just wagging their tails at the quality of wine they can produce from Lake County winegrapes.

Aliénor Cellars

OWNER / HISTORY

May-Britt Malbec, winemaking consultant, and Bonnie & David Weiss, farming consultants, started Aliénor as the result of a "vibrant friendship," which later transformed into a very "sophisticated" collaboration.

AVA / ELEVATION

Average about 1,400 feet from the Big Valley AVA.

WINEMAKER

May-Britt Malbec

VARIETALS GROWN

Cabernet Franc, Petit Verdot, Merlot, Syrah, Cabernet Sauvignon, Sauvignon Blanc.

WINES PRODUCED

Approximately 1,500 cases annually;
Aliénor Grand Vin (Bordeaux style red)
Aliénor Le Roseraie
Aliénor Sauvignon Blanc
Aliénor Late Harvest Sauvignon Blanc
Aliénor Cotes de Castelero

The Aliénor range of wines began in 2005 as a joint venture between the proprietor Malbec and Weiss families. May-Britt is the Aliénor winemaker and is a consultant with impeccable credentials: She was one of the very best sommeliers in the Nordic countries before moving to France in 1995 to oversee Public Relations for Chateau Latour. It was at Latour (one of *the* very best Chateaux in Bordeaux) that May-Britt met her late husband Denis Malbec, who was born there as his father Jean-Noël was the Cellar Master. In 2000 the Malbecs decided to pursue a consulting career, which led them to America. The Bella Vista Farming Company owned by Bonnie and David Weiss is a long-established, highly respected consulting firm who develop and manage a large number of prime vineyards throughout the county.

TEL: 707-963-9606 or 707-318-3112
EMAIL: contact@alienorwines.com

Art+Farm Wine

OWNER / HISTORY
Kat & Rob McDonald started the business in 2003.

AVA / ELEVATION
Cabernet is grown in the Amber Knolls vineyard, Red Hills, at between 2,000 and 2,400 ft. The Sauvignon Blanc is grown in Rooster Vineyard in Big Valley at 1,400 ft.

WINEMAKERS
The McDonalds have a rich wine history, in both Australia and the US.

VARIETALS GROWN
Cabernet Sauvignon & Sauvignon Blanc.

WINES PRODUCED
The "girls in the vineyard" is their label for single varietal, single vineyard in a single season wines. The Cabernet Sauvignon and Sauvignon Blanc are from Lake County. They make other blends. A donation to charity is made with each purchase.

Kat and Rob McDonald have been making and selling wine for 20 years. Rob grew up in Australia's famed Adelaide Hills wine region. In the 1990s they started a company to introduce Americans to the high quality, family-owned Australian wines that they knew and loved. They kept a foot on Australian terroir, however, establishing a dry-grown, naturally-farmed vineyard in the Heathcote, Victoria area of the country. In 2003 they decided to farm land in California and bought a prized Napa Valley Cabernet vineyard, collaborating with many great winemakers in Australia and New Zealand to make a very highly-regarded set of wines. They soon discovered another source of ultra-premium winegrapes on their doorstep, in Lake County. Their delicious Sauvignon Blanc and Cabernet Sauvignon wines are from Lake's grapes.

TEL: 707-927-4343 WEB: www.artfarmwine.com
EMAIL: grow@artfarmwine.com

Bodkin

OWNER / HISTORY
Chris Christensen/WeFew Vintners LLC.

AVA / ELEVATION
Sauvignon Blanc at 1,140 ft.

WINEMAKER
Chris Christensen worked at 9 different wineries in 12 years before opening Bodkin. As an African-America wine-maker he continues a long tradition that stretches back to Monticello.

LAKE COUNTY VARIETALS
Sauvignon Blanc, Musqué Clone, Muscat Canelli, Zinfandel

WINES PRODUCED
Sparkling Sauvignon Blanc, Sauvignon Blanc, and skin-fermented Sauvignon Blanc, are 75% from Lake County grapes. The dry Muscat Canelli is a vineyard-designated wine from Sandy Bend. Bodkin Wines have received eleven 90+ point scores, and two Editors' Choice awards from the *Wine Enthusiast* magazine.

Chris Christensen named his wines after the 1415 battle of Agincourt, in which outnumbered English archers defeated the French using bodkin-type arrowheads. Originally from Iowa, Chris spent 8 years studying winemaking in Australia. In 2011 he started Bodkin Wines in California. The first wine-maker in the USA to produce a sparkling Sauvignon Blanc, his *Cuvée Agincourt Brut*, is his pride and joy. Bodkin showcases Sauvignon Blanc's versatility as a sparkling wine; an off-dry, citrusy, floral still wine; and a late harvest dessert wine. He also makes a "seriously dry" Muscat Canelli. He believes Lake County grapes lend themselves to a Sauvignon Blanc more like those of Austria or New Zealand: austere, understated, textural, lower alcohol, higher acidity, limited new oak, and maximum finesse. Drink these wines and enjoy life in the spirit of the Bodkin Wines motto, "We few. We happy few".

TEL: 707-291-8863 WEB: www.bodkinwines.com
EMAIL: chris@bodkinwines.com

Cougar's Leap

OWNER / HISTORY
Purchased in 2008 by Nils Venge

AVA / ELEVATION
Ranges from 2,200-2,400 ft.

WINEMAKER
Nils has 45 years experience in wine-making. As Winemaker and General Manager for Groth Winery in Napa, he received a 100-point score for a re-serve Cabernet Sauvignon from Robert Parker, Jr., the first American to do so.

VARIETALS GROWN
Petite Syrah and Zinfandel, plus some small production field blends.

WINES PRODUCED
Petite Syrah, Zinfandel, Cougar's Cuvée (Zinfandel and Tempranillo), Wild Cat Red (Cabernet Sauvignon, Merlot, Cab Franc, and Syrah), Wild Cat White (Sémillion and Sauvignon Blanc), and a Late Harvest Zinfandel.

Nils Venge arrived in the Napa Valley in 1970, his passion for winemaking soon earning him the title of the "King of Cabernet." Famous wine critic Robert M. Parker, Jr. awarded Nils a 100-point score for a Reserve Cabernet Sauvignon, the first American to be awarded this high a rating on Parker's 50-100 point scale. His philosophy on making wines is that they must reflect the best qualities that the fruit has to offer. In 2008 Nils Venge purchased his Black Rock Ranch in the Red Hills AVA. The ranch is named after the large deposits of shiny obsidian rock exposed throughout the volcanic soils. Planting of the vineyard began in 1995. The head-pruned vines yield a hearty grape and Nils is thrilled with the color and intensity that the wine has delivered from the Red Hills Appellation.

TEL: 707-326-9812 **WEB**: www.cougarsleap.com
EMAIL: info@cougarsleap.com

Dancing Crow Vineyards

OWNER / HISTORY
The 36-acre Vineyard in the Big Valley AVA was purchased in 2013 by Tony Cartlidge and Sarah Forni-Cartlidge. Sons Adam Forni and Stefan Cartlidge also run the family business.

AVA / ELEVATION
Sauvignon Blanc is from Big Valley AVA. Various Lake County Reds, including a Rhône-style blend and a Cabernet Sauvignon from the Red Hills and High Valley AVAs.

WINEMAKERS
David and Katharine DeSante have made wines in the US, France, and Australia's Margaret River region, which is known for Sauvignon Blanc.

VARIETALS GROWN
30 acres of Sauvignon Blanc (Certified California Sustainable Winegrowing).

WINES PRODUCED
Approximately 4,500 cases of Dancing Crow Sauvignon Blanc and 4,000 cases of Dancing Crow Cabernet Sauvignon, all produced from Lake County Grapes.

The Forni-Cartlidge Family have a long pedigree in the California wine industry. Four generations of Forni Winemakers stretch back to 1903, with Charles Forni helping to found the first Napa Valley Vintners Association. Tony Cartlidge, the driving force behind Dancing Crow, also has a distinguished wine career, developing the 120,000 case Cartlidge & Browne Win-ery, which produced and distributed award-winning wines globally. In 2004 Tony bought some Dancing Crow Vineyard grapes from Lake County to produce a vineyard designate wine, which was extremely well received. When the vineyards became available for sale Tony and family decided the time had come to follow their dream and produce their own wine. With local viticulturist David Weiss, and veteran winemakers David and Katharine DeSante on board, they set about creating a very unique style of Sauvignon Blanc, more in the style of a French Sancerre, which is getting much critical acclaim. They also produce a great Red Hills and High Valley AVA Cabernet Sauvignon.

TEL: 707-287-4495 **WEB**: dancingcrow.com
EMAIL: tony@dancingcrowvineyards.com

Obsidian Ridge

The vineyards which are situated on the Mayacamas Mountains, at between 2,340-2,875 ft., are among the highest in the North Coast. The Molnar family began planting vines in Napa in the late 1960s. When they saw an abandoned Lake County walnut orchard on young volcanic gravels, shot-through with obsidian, they were convinced that the Red Hills "were the new frontier of premium Cabernet Sauvignon in California." High elevation, with its more intense UV light and later season cooling, produces grapes with "mountain intensity and structure balanced with generous fruit." The 2017 expansion, adding 140 acres, allowed a wider range of Cabernet Sauvignon clones to be blended with Bordeaux varietals. Each vintage is aged for 18 months+ in extremely tight grained oak from Northern Hungary where the family owns and manages the Kádár cooperage. Oak from this volcanic region is very aromatic lifting the brighter and purer notes of mountain fruit.

TEL: 707-255-4929 WEB: www.obsidianridge.com
EMAIL: mail@obsidianridge.com

OWNER / HISTORY
Established in 2003 with 3 founding partners: Arpad Molnar, Peter Molnar, and Michael Blaise Terrien.

AVA / ELEVATION
Red Hills AVA between 2,340-2,875 ft.

WINEMAKERS
Alex Beloz has been the winemaker for the past twelve vintages. Michael Terrien, the founding winemaker, studied Enology at UC Davis. While a student, in 1995 he began experimenting with Pinot on the Molnar family vineyards–the start of a long collaboration.

VARIETALS GROWN
240 acres of Cabernet Sauvignon, Petite Sirah, Petit Verdot, Malbec and Merlot.

WINES PRODUCED
The wines are all single vineyard wines, but they have also identified specific "sweet spots" (and resultant wines) within individual vineyards. The Cabernets are: *Obsidian Ridge*,15,200 cases; *Half Mile*, 325 cases; *Obsidian Ridge "The Slope,"* 250 cases.

R Vineyards

Monica and David Rosenthal have been involved in the wine industry for over 30 years. David's parents purchased 100 acres of land in the Middletown area in the early 1970s. The property already had a 20-acre vineyard on it with some old Zinfandel vines dating back to the 1930s. They have expanded the vineyard considerably, but still make wine from those old Zinfandel vines. David's first harvest as winemaker was in the county in 1980. Later, working for Buena Vista, David had the opportunity to study with legendary winemaker André Tchelistcheff, credited by many to have transformed Northern California into a world-class winemaking region. Fans of their Viognier have long suggested they start their own label–now they have! They are ably assisted by son Russell and 3 vine dogs.

TEL: 707-355-2762 or 707-987-2760 WEB: rvineyards.com
EMAIL: RVineyards@sonic.net or viognier@sonic.net

OWNER / HISTORY
Monica and David Rosenthal released their first wines under their R Vineyards label in 2014.

AVA / ELEVATION
Vineyards are on the north slope of Mt. St. Helena, part of the Mayacamas Mountain range, at 1,100 ft. elevation.

WINEMAKER
David has a degree in winemaking from UC Davis. He has made wine for many wineries. Today he is the winemaker for the Yokayo Wine Co.

VARIETALS GROWN
Viognier (10 acres), Cabernet Franc (2.5), Cabernet Sauvignon (7.5), Old Vine Zinfandel (3), and some Petite Sirah and Syrah.

WINES PRODUCED
50-200 cases annually: Viognier, a Bordeaux style red wine blend, Cabernet Franc, and Old Vine Zinfandel.

Tejada Vineyard Company

OWNER / HISTORY

The land was purchased in 1999 by Celia, Ibo, and Nina Tejada, and the vineyard planted in 2000.

AVA / ELEVATION

Vineyards are in the Upper Lake area at an average elevation of 1,450 ft.

WINEMAKERS

Byron Kosuge and Pat Knittel have worked with the Tejadas to evolve a winemaking process best suited to the Tempranillo from their vineyard. The wine is very gently handled "almost like Pinot Noir" and is then taken off the skins quite early and then racked only once during its 16 months in barrel.

VARIETALS GROWN

There are 4.75 acres under vine, 75% Tempranillo, 25% Garnacha.

WINES PRODUCED

100 cases annually of *Tejada Reserve*, a Spanish-style Tempranillo blend.

Celia Tejada and her brother, Ibo, were raised in a small mountain village called Ruerrero in Northern Spain. Later when both siblings found themselves in California pursuing busy careers–Celia in interior and product design and Ibo in building restoration–they decided to establish a country ranch where both families could relax. They love to share all aspects of their Spanish heritage and culture with friends and family, particularly food and wine traditions. The idyllic country ranch in Upper Lake also provided the perfect place to start their own vineyard. Naturally they decided to plant famous Spanish varietals: Tempranillo and Garnacha, which they found thrived on the rocky soils found in Upper Lake. They took the time to experiment in developing their winemaking processes. The grapes are carefully crafted into a wine that best expresses the Tejadas' ranch site and Spanish roots.

TEL: 510-231-6930 **WEB:** www.tejadavines.com
EMAIL: info@tejadavines.com

Two Angels

OWNERS / HISTORY

The Kreps Family started the label.

AVAS / ELEVATION

2,000 feet.

WINEMAKERS

Consulting winemaker Robert Pepi studied winemaking at UC Davis's renowned Enology program and at The Wine Lab in St. Helena. He has amassed nearly four decades of experience in winemaking around the world, from his own Robert Pepi Wines in Napa to Bodega Valentin Bianchi in Mendoza, Argentina. As winemaker, he creates wines that are "fruity", balanced, and complex.

VARIETALS GROWN

Sauvignon Blanc and Petit Sirah.

WINES PRODUCED

Sauvignon Blanc and Petit Sirah. These excellent, sought-after wines have attracted much critical acclaim and will be available for purchase at the Lake County Wine Studio.

Two Angels wines are heavenly with "California character". Legend has it that when a wine is truly celestial, the angels secretly fly down to taste it, taking the "Angel's Share"–this accounts for wine lost during in-barrel aging. International winemaker Robert Pepi creates ultra-premium wines, "true to their terroir, yet affordable." He brings almost 40 years of experience to the endeavor. For 10 years he was winemaker and general manager of Robert Pepi Wines which he co-owned with his father, producing best-selling, highly-rated wines, notably Sauvignon Blanc, Sangiovese, and Cabernet Sauvignon. In 1994 when the label was sold he started traveling the world as a highly sought-after consultant. His prestigious clients have included wineries such as Andretti in Napa and as far away as Valentin Bianchi in Argentina. Using Lake County's ultra-premium grapes, he has crafted some (more affordable) but equally highly-regarded wines: a fruit-forward Sauvignon Blanc and an intense, luxurious, Petite Sirah.

TEL: 707-226-8300 **WEB**: www.quintessentialwines.

Lady of the Lake Sparkling Pear Wine

The Lake County pear industry was once world-renowned and, at its height, spawned some truly charming fruit-crate graphics. When the industry declined in the 1980s, a bright idea was hatched by the Mt. Konocti families (*see Owners*), to turn local pears into a 'Pear Champagne.' This successful venture was matched with the equally clever idea to adopt the original 1926 pear crate label (*above*) as the the Lady of the Lake label – a fitting homage to the industry. *Lady of the Lake* is made in exactly the same way as classic French Champagne. The freshly-picked pears are sent to be juiced at a crush facility in Sebastapol, a nearby apple growing region, with stronger presses than those used for grapes. The juice then returns to Mt. Konocti for the traditional 'méthode champenoise' process of riddling and disgorgement. Santé!

OWNERS / HISTORY

The producers of this Lake County speciality are the Gayaldo, Carpenter and Oldham Families. These 3 Lake County pear farming families were all part of the original Mt. Konocti Growers Cooperative. In the 1980s, when pear farming was in its heyday, the cooperative had over 68 members.

ELEVATION/ AVA

Pears in Lake County are usually farmed on the valley floor at about 1,400 feet. Many pear orchards are located in the Big Valley wine AVA.

WINEMAKING PROCESS

The freshly picked pears are sent to be juiced at a crush facility in Sebastapol, a traditional apple growing region with stronger presses. The juice is returned to Mt. Konocti for the traditional 'méthode champenoise' processing of riddling and disgorgement.

VARIETALS GROWN

This product is a blend of popular Lake County pear varietals – Bartlet (80%) and Bosc (20%) – a special cuvée that has been perfected over the years.

WINES PRODUCED

2,000 cases currently, more planned.

Top: The original 1926 pear-crate artwork that was adapted for the Lady of the Lake sparkling Pear wine. Left: More examples of crate graphics. Above: A collection of 1950s worker's cars outside the thriving Mt. Konocti Growers' Cooperatvive.

TEL: 707-279-4213 **WEB:** www.mtkonoctiwines.com **EMAIL:** robert@mtkonoctiwines.com

Learning about Wine at the Tallman Hotel

Built in 1896 after a fire destroyed its predecessor, the Tallman Hotel in Upper Lake was originally a stage stop and popular gathering spot before falling into disrepair and disuse in the 1960s. It has now been immaculately restored by Lynne & Bernie Butcher and it is listed on the California Register of Historic Places. The adjoining Blue Wing Saloon has also been brought back to life by the Butchers, quite literally. This is *the* local hot-spot for live music (and popular music festivals) in the county. The restaurant's wine list is composed exclusively of fine local wines. The hotel is, handily, directly opposite the Lake County Wine Studio.

SPECIAL EVENTS AT THE TALLMAN

Lake County has many excellent chefs, attracted by the county's abundance of fresh local produce, incredible wines, and the many farmers raising grass-fed animals (including a local bison farm). The Tallman Hotel hosts a variety of special events each year featuring guest chefs and local winemakers. They collaborate to create menus that best showcase their selection of wines. The chefs prepare dishes using many local seasonal ingredients. These small popular gatherings are held in the elegantly restored Tallman dining room. The winemakers introduce and describe each pairing and happily answer questions.

Road Scholars at the Tallman

Road Scholar, Inc. is a global non-profit education program focused on the curious traveler. The Tallman's Lake County Wine Program is specially designed for Road Scholars. The 5-day programs are held in the spring (at bud break) and fall (for harvest time). They are designed to showcase this rapidly emerging, but not yet overly commercialized, wine region. Lake County is still a place where the local vineyard owners and winemakers who teach the course are available to enthusiastically share their knowledge and passion with visitors. *More information at: https://www.roadscholar.org*

North of Napa: Wine Country the Way it Used to Be

The 5-day course is a mixture of lectures and hands-on experience. The many excursions to different vineyards and winery sites will provide a thorough understanding of winemaking in the county. Topics include:

- The history of Lake County, its wineries, and the industry today
- An introduction to the extraordinary local geology, topography, soils, and terroir
- An explanation of the county AVAs and appellations with a leading local winemaker
- Visits to a number of wineries with different viticulture and winemaking practices
- The winemaking process from vine to bottle
- A hands-on wine blending contest
- Guided food and wine pairings with local chefs using local produce

Lake County Olive Oils

- The program also includes a visit to the Chacewater Winery, which is the county's premier producer of different varietal olive oils.

White Wine Varietals

Many white wine varietals grow here that you might not expect from a region with such hot, sunny summers. Again, this is thanks to the unique climatic conditions found in Lake County. The high altitude, cooling effects of the lake, and the colder evening temperatures all serve to cool the grapes down at the end of each day and preserve important acidity levels in the fruit. Sauvignon Blanc is one of the most popular white varietals (see opposite), but many other traditionally cooler climate varietals thrive. Riesling and Gewürztraminer can grow very well here, typically at higher elevations or with close proximity to the lake and its constant breezes. Some winemakers also make wines using winegrapes from adjoining regions, which adds to the great range of wines available to taste in Lake County.

SAUVIGNON BLANC

In France the Sauvignon Blanc grape has been grown for centuries in areas that also have considerable Cabernet Sauvignon vineyards, and the same is true In Lake County! This grape varietal is used to make Sancerre and Pouilly-Fumé. It is often blended with Sémillon in Bordeaux. Fumé Blanc (a Robert Mondavi creation) is when Sauvignon Blanc is exposed to oak.

WINE STYLE
Typically a lighter-bodied crisp style wine with good acidity. Refreshing and zesty. Typically designed to be drunk when young. Lake County growing conditions offer many possible styles of Sauvignon Blanc, and local winemakers are masters at perfecting the fruit to acidity balance.

TYPICAL FLAVORS
Grass • Herbs • Citrus • Green Apple Grapefruit • Lemongrass • Green Tea Mango • Papaya • Pineapple.

GOOD WITH
Salads, fish and shellfish, especially oysters, citrus and tomato sauces, goat cheese; one of the few wines that can pair well with asparagus.

PINOT GRIGIO (GRIS)

The Italian name for the Pinot Gris varietal of French origins. It is widely planted in northeastern Italy, notably in the Friuli-Venetia region. The Italian style Pinot Grigio tends to be a very clean, crisp and dry style of wine. As "Pinot Gris," in the Alsace region of France, it is a popular wine with a similar crisp acidity, but is crafted into a fruitier, more aromatic style of wine.

WINE STYLE
Generally a lighter crisp style wine, sometimes with a very slight musty flavor. Usually best drunk when young. A good range of Pinot Grigios from quite dry to more fruity can be tasted in the county. The winemakers' vision for where on this spectrum their wine should go is all part of the fun!

TYPICAL FLAVORS
Melon • Apple • Citrus • Lemon Pear • Nuts • Honey • Smoky, minerally accent is sometimes to be found associated with this varietal.

GOOD WITH
Shellfish, salmon and smoked salmon, chicken, pâté, charcuterie, quiches, onion tart, mushroom dishes, goat cheeses and slightly spicy foods.

RIESLING

This famous German grape varietal was once forbidden to be grown more than 30 miles from the German border by the French wine police! Some feel Gallic rivalry rather than cool climate kept this wine so firmly associated with Germany in the "old world." Lake County has been growing this grape for 150 years. It grows well here due to high altitudes with cooler nights.

WINE STYLE
An aromatic light to medium-bodied style wine with a soft delicate floral aroma and good acidity. A versatile grape varietal that can be made into a drier or a rather fruity style wine. Many styles of Riesling can be tasted in the region. Johannisberg Riesling was one of the earliest grapes grown here.

TYPICAL FLAVORS
Honey • Apricot • Peach • Pear Quince • Passion Fruit • Spiced Baked Apples • Flowers • Delicate but distinct aromatic quality, can even verge towards a slightly perfumed scent.

GOOD WITH
Often a recommended choice to pair with Asian and ethnic foods, and meats with sweet sauces such as BBQ.

Sauvignon Blanc in Lake County

The most planted white wine grape in the county–with good reason –as it loves it here. It is prized by the neighboring wine regions of Napa and Sonoma, where it has long been a key component in many prestigious Sauvignon Blanc labels. The last two decades have seen a big influx of wineries establishing themselves in Lake County, attracted by the unique climate and soils. This shift to winemaking has attracted many talented winemakers who are making award -winning wines with Lake County labels on the bottles. Sauvignon Blanc is one of the wines at which the county excels. Local growers are masters at managing the canopy of this prolific varietal so that it can be pushed towards a typical tart, grassy, herbaceous style of wine or, by allowing more sun to reach the grapes, some nice tropical fruit flavors can be achieved. Balancing such choices is the art of fine winemaking for which the county is becoming famous.

VIOGNIER

A trickier-to-grow varietal which may have traveled to France from the Dalmatian Coast, courtesy of the Roman Empire back in 281 AD. Established in Condrieu appellation in the Northern Rhône. Once a less-grown and lesser-known winegrape, it has steadily grown in popularity and now has many devotees who relish this lush, slightly exotic wine style with or without food.

WINE STYLE

A richer medium to full-bodied style of wine with some intriguing exotic flower aromas, such as freesia, jasmine, or oleander. At its best has a lush fruit quality without being overly sweet. Sometimes is exposed to oak. Typically has a smooth creamy mouth feel.

TYPICAL FLAVORS

Ripe Apricot • Ripe Pear • Violets Honeysuckle • Jasmine • Gardenia Fig • White Peaches • Mango • Vanilla Lush and exotically aromatic; can also have a hint of spiciness.

GOOD WITH

Seafood such as scallops, grilled fish, and poultry. Can be paired with richer buttery or cream based sauces. Pairs particularly well with Thai food.

CHARDONNAY

Classic French varietal famous for White Burgundy and Champagne. Beloved by viticulturists for its ease to cultivate and by winemakers for its great malleability. It can be manipulated so many ways that it can be hard to make generalizations with so many styles available. Use of, and length of time in, oak barrels as well as winemaker choices about malolactic fermentation and contact with lees are all key to the final wine style.

WINE STYLE

Depending on how the wine is handled, particularly the length of exposure to oak barrels, the wine can be anything from medium to very full-bodied. Often a more viscous and golden colored wine. The distinct buttery taste, a creamy mouth feel accompanied by rich, ripe fruit flavors are some common characteristics.

TYPICAL FLAVORS

Citrus • Pear • Banana • Peach • Honey Pineapple • Tropical Fruits • Thyme Toast • Butter • Vanilla • Wax • Nuts Often a buttery, ripe fruit, richer wine.

GOOD WITH

Richer dishes with buttery or creamy sauces. Risotto, game, salmon, lobster, crab, Gorgonzola, fruit desserts.

MUSCAT

Another of the grape varietals widely planted in Lake County back in the 1870s. Its roots go way deeper than this, however, as it may have been the first vine that the ancient Greeks took to France. In Italy it is made into a light sparking wine called Moscato d'Asti. Here it is generally made into what Aussies call a "stickie," a sweet dessert wine. Interestingly, one of the few wines that actually tastes of fresh grapes!

WINE STYLE

Many Lake County wineries offer a good range of wines, including dessert wines, which can be an exciting finale to the tasting room experience. Muscat Canelli and Orange Muscat are popular dessert wines found in the county. Others are "Late Harvest" wines where the grapes have been left on the vine longer than normal to develop a lush rich sweetness.

TYPICAL FLAVORS

Grapes • Oranges • Roses • Dried Fruit Caramel • Fig • Honey • Pineapple Pear • Prune • Hazelnut

GOOD WITH

Sweet desserts such as pecan pie, chocolate, and depending on the style, even orange or ginger desserts.

Red Wine Varietals

The unique volcanic soils and mountain climate of Lake County are perfect terroir for a great range of red wine varietals, which tend to be planted at the higher elevations (1,600-3,000 feet). The stronger UV light found at these elevations triggers the skins to protect the seeds inside, creating the prized "mountain fruit," which has smaller berries, thicker skins, and more concentrated intense fruit flavor. The mineral rich soils, hot summer days and cool evenings produce exceptional quality fruit. The resulting award-winning wines are attracting serious critical acclaim. The variety of excellent red wines coming from Lake County is testament to a fresh, dynamic, and creative winemaking culture that has emerged in the last few years, which offers wine travelers an exceptional selection of fine red wines.

GRENACHE (GARNACHA)

This popular Northern Spanish grape varietal soon made its way over the Pyrenees into Languedoc, Provence, and the Rhône. In both Spain and France it is a popular grape for making Rosé or Rosada. It is often blended with Tempranillo in Spain to make robust Rioja wines. In southern Rhône it is part of the Châteauneuf du Pape and Côtes du Rhône blends. In California it has become a popular elegant, fruity and slightly spicy wine.

WINE STYLE

As a single varietal red wine Grenache is typically a juicy, fruity wine with a slightly spicy quality. In Lake County examples range from medium to more full-bodied and the fruit forwardness is balanced with good acidity and soft tannins, allowing them to pair well with a wide range of foods.

TYPICAL FLAVORS

Raspberry • Strawberry • Cherry White Pepper • Cinnamon • Spice

GOOD WITH

Spanish tapas, grilled and roasted lighter meats such as pork, chicken, and turkey. Also, Mediterranean dishes with pasta, fresh herbs or garlic.

SYRAH

In the northern Rhône Syrah is the only red grape varietal allowed by law to carry the name of that appellation. In the southern Rhône it is also made into a single varietal Rosé. The northern Rhône Syrahs are big, earthy, and fruity. In Australia the grape is known as Shiraz, where it is made into bolder, "jammy," intensely concentrated wines with pronounced pepper and spice. Lake County winemakers make Syrah wines in a great range of styles.

WINE STYLE

A lively wine with a lot of highly concentrated fruit flavors that can be quite intense. These are often big, gutsy wines with dark fruit flavors, deep color, and often with an interesting slight musky, dusty quality.

TYPICAL FLAVORS

Plum • Blackberry • Red Berries Cherry • Dark Chocolate • Mocha • Tar Pepper • Smoke • Musk • Vanilla

GOOD WITH

Roast lamb, game, braised meat dishes, casseroles and ragus. Dishes that have stronger flavors. Hearty comfort foods such as lasagna, moussaka, sausages, beans, and lentils.

PETITE SIRAH

This grape has been cited as the "Durif" grape varietal, named after a French doctor who propagated it in 1880 by crossing the Syrah grape with a varietal called Peloursin. Whether true or not, it's "Petite Sirah" in its new American home. It is a popular wine in Lake County and has the intense dark fruit of Syrah, plus an even more pronounced dark, inky, purple color and distinct spiciness. It is sometimes used in blending to add extra structure and color.

WINE STYLE

These are big, heavy-bodied wines with tannins and the ability to age well. They are deep, inky, purple colored wines and are widely enjoyed for their luscious blackcurrant, jammy fruit flavors. Typical characteristics are also spicy and peppery notes.

TYPICAL FLAVORS

Blackberry • Blackcurrant • Prune Blueberry • Black Pepper • Black Cherry Licorice • Spice • Violet •

GOOD WITH

Big meaty dishes such as braised short ribs. Rich stews, game, strong flavors such as pepperoni, roquefort and blue cheese. BBQ and spicy sauces.

Cabernet Sauvignon in Lake County

For centuries world-famous wines from the Cabernet Sauvignon grape hailed largely from the Bordeaux region of France. In the late nineteenth century Lillie Langry made her own "Claret" at the Guenoc Ranch in Lake County. When Robert Mondavi led the charge to create world-class wines in California in the mid 1960s, Lake County growers were there ready to supply Cabernet Sauvignon grapes to him. Many Lake County Cabernet grapes have traveled over the Mayacamas mountains in the last 50 years to become part of prestigious Napa Valley Cabernets. The return to winemaking *inside* the county has seen a marked increase in momentum in the last 10-15 years, and wines have emerged that have shone a spotlight on the quality of the region's Cabernets. World-renowned winemakers have come into the county specifically to make Cabernets. The unique terroir in Lake County is producing sophisticated, bold, intense, complex, well-structured Cabernets of the finest quality.

MERLOT

The wine regions of the Pomerol and St.-Emilion in France are famous for their Merlot wines. Merlot became a popular single varietal wine in California as it's a slightly softer, smooth, fruity quality wine that is great paired with food. The softer tannins mean it can be drunk much younger than a typical Cabernet Sauvignon wine.

WINE STYLE
A supple, softer, fruity, smooth medium-bodied red wine which has a reputation for being an easy drinking wine, and one that pairs well with food. Often has quite intense concentrated fruit flavors and a sweet spiciness with a velvety dark chocolate feel.

TYPICAL FLAVORS
Blueberry • Raspberry • Blackberry Damson Plums • Black Cherry Dark Chocolate • Tobacco • Clove Vanilla • Green Tea • Mocha

GOOD WITH
Grilled meats and poultry, meatier fish such as tuna, Mediterranean dishes with herbs and garlic, prosciutto. Chocolate desserts.

CABERNET SAUVIGNON

One of the most famous and admired red grape varietals in the old and new worlds. It is the basis for many of the world's great wines. The grape is relatively easy to grow, has a lot of fruit and typically plenty of tannins which enable the wines to age. With time the tannins mellow and complex flavors get layered into the wine. Merlot, Cabernet Franc, and Petit Verdot are often blended with it to smooth out some of its natural robustness. Lake County Cabs spend many months aging in French, American, and Hungarian oak barrels to further refine the wine before bottling.

WINE STYLE
A full-bodied, long-lived wine with great potential to improve with age, though many wines are also made to be drunk when young. Has excellent ripe fruit flavor, complexity, and plenty of tannins.

TYPICAL FLAVORS
Blackberry • Plum • Toasty Oak • Dark Chocolate • Blackcurrants • Vanilla • Fig Spices • Black Tea • Bell Pepper

GOOD WITH
Red meats, pepper steak, marinated meats, chargrilled meats. Rack of lamb, bolognese. Mushroom dishes.

ZINFANDEL

The Zinfandel grape was for many years the grape California was most known for by the rest of the world. Certainly it was among the most popular varietals to be planted by early Lake County winemakers. There are some 100-year-old vines in the county that still bear fruit and are making wonderful "Old Vine" Zinfandels. Some local winemakers choose to blend it with a small amount of Petite Sirah.

WINE STYLE
Depending on how ripe the grapes are when picked and the time it is exposed to oak barrels, the wine can be anything from medium to very full-bodied. It is a brambly fruit wine with a deep color, generally having fewer tannins than, say, Cabernet. It is thought to be related to Primitivo and is a great wine to enjoy with Italian style food.

TYPICAL FLAVORS
Plum • Blackberry • Strawberry Cedar • Bramble • Black Pepper Cinnamon • Nutmeg • Clove • Jam

GOOD WITH
Cioppino, duck, roasted meats, barbequed meats, chilli con carne, pizza; can be paired with dishes with slightly sweeter sauces. Chocolate.

A-Z of Lake County Winegrapes and Wine Styles

An amazing range of grape varietals thrive in Lake's unique terroir. The vast majority listed are grown locally–all are then carefully crafted by county winemakers. Many less common varietals are made in small lots, some can only be enjoyed by visiting the winery. The vast selection of wine styles, offers the adventurous wine enthusiast plenty of fine choices.

WINEMAKER BLENDS
In addition to the huge selection of award-winning single varietal wines, many wineries also have excellent blends and cuveés reflecting the local winemakers'skill, and sheer creativity.

Aglianico
Rosa d'Oro Vineyards, 88

Albariño
Fore Family Vineyards, 68

Aligoté
Steele Wines, 100

Barbera
Kaz/Lakeport Winery, 76
Olof Cellars, 86
Rosa d'Oro Vineyards, 88
Shannon Ridge Family of Wines, 90
Shed Horn Cellars, 92
Smiling Dogs Ranch, 96
Steele Wines, 100

Blaufränkisch
Steele Wines, 100

Cabernet Franc
Aliénor Cellars, 110
Beaver Creek Vineyards, 54
Chacewater Winery 64
Cougars Leap Winery, 112
Hawk and Horse Vineyards, 74
Langtry Estate & Vineyards, 78
Laujor Estate, 80
R Vineyards, 113
Shannon Ridge Family of Wines, 90
Sol Rouge Winery, 98
Steele Wines, 100

Cabernet Sauvignon
Aliénor Cellars, 110
Art+Farm Wine, 111
Beaver Creek Vineyards, 54
Boatique Winery, 56
Brassfield Estate Winery, 58
Bullion Creek Vineyards, 60
Cache Creek Vineyards, 62
Chacewater Winery, 64
Cougar's Leap, 112
Dancing Crow Vineyards, 112
Don Angel Cellars, 66
Fore Family Vineyards, 68
Fults Family Vineyards, 70
Gregory Graham Wines, 72
Hawk and Horse Vineyards, 74
Kaz/Lakeport Winery, 76
Langtry Estate & Vineyards, 78
Mt. Konocti Winery, 82
Noggle Vineyards & Winery, 84
Obsidian Ridge, 113
R Vineyards, 113
Shannon Ridge Family of Wines, 90
Shed Horn Cellars, 92

Six Sigma Ranch & Winery, 94
Smiling Dogs Ranch, 96
Sol Rouge Winery, 98
Steele Wines, 100
Stonehouse Cellars, 102
Thorn Hill Vineyards, 104
Wildhurst Vineyards, 106

Cabernet Sauv. dessert wine
Hawk and Horse Vineyards, 74

Charbono
Bullion Creek Vineyards, 60

Chardonnay
Cache Creek Vineyards, 62
Chacewater Winery, 64
Don Angel Cellars, 66
Fults Family Vineyards, 70
Gregory Graham Wines, 72
Langtry Estate & Vineyards, 78
Shannon Ridge Family of Wines, 90
Shed Horn Cellars, 92
Steele Wines, 100
Thorn Hill Vineyards, 104
Wildhurst Vineyards, 106

Cinsaut /Cinsault
Shannon Ridge Family of Wines, 90
Sol Rouge Winery, 98

Counoise
Sol Rouge Winery, 98
Steele Wines, 100

Dolcetto
Rosa d'Oro Vineyards, 88

Gewürztraminer
Brassfield Estate Winery, 58

Grenache (Garnacha)
Brassfield Estate Winery, 58
Fore Family Vineyards (G.Blanc), 68
Fore Family Vineyards (G.Noir), 68
Fults Family Vineyards, 70
Gregory Graham Wines, 72
Shannon Ridge Family of Wines, 90
Shed Horn Cellars, 92
Sol Rouge Winery, 98
Steele Wines, 100
Stonehouse Cellars, 102
Tejada Vineyard Company, 114

Lenoir
Kaz/Lakeport Winery, 76
Olof Cellars, 86

Malbec
Boatique Winery, 56

Brassfield Estate Winery, 58
Chacewater Winery, 64
Don Angel Cellars, 66
Fults Family Vineyards, 70
Langtry Estate & Vineyards, 78
Laujor Estate, 80
Obsidian Ridge, 113
Olof Cellars, 86
Shannon Ridge Family of Wines, 90
Steele Wines, 100

Marsanne
Langtry Estate & Vineyards, 78

Merlot
Aliénor Cellars, 110
Chacewater Winery, 64
Cougars Leap Winery, 112
Fore Family Vineyards, 68
Kaz/Lakeport Winery, 76
Obsidian Ridge, 113
Shannon Ridge Family of Wines, 90
Six Sigma Ranch & Winery, 94
Smiling Dogs Ranch, 96
Steele Wines, 100
Stonehouse Cellars, 102
Thorn Hill Vineyards, 104
Wildhurst Vineyards, 106

Montepulciano
Don Angel Cellars, 66
Rosa d'Oro Vineyards, 88

Mourvèdre
Brassfield Estate Winery, 58
Fore Family Vineyards, 68
Shannon Ridge Family of Wines, 90
Sol Rouge Winery, 98

Muscat
Mt. Konocti Winery, 82
Rosa d'Oro Vineyards, 88
Wildhurst Vineyards, 106

Moscato
Brassfield Estate Winery, 58
Fults Family Vineyards, 70
Gregory Graham Wines, 72

Muscat Canelli
Chacewater Winery 64
Don Angel Cellars, 66

Orange Muscat
Don Angel Cellars, 66

Nebbiolo
Olof Cellars, 86
Rosa d'Oro Vineyards, 88

Negroamaro
Rosa d'Oro Vineyards, 88

Petite Sirah
Beaver Creek Vineyards, 54
Brassfield Estate Winery, 58
Cache Creek Vineyards, 62
Chacewater Winery, 64
Don Angel Cellars, 66
Fults Family Vineyards, 70
Gregory Graham Wines, 72
Hawk and Horse Vineyards, 74
Kaz/Lakeport Winery, 76
Langtry Estate & Vineyards, 78
Laujor Estate, 80
Obsidian Ridge, 113
R Vineyards, 113
Shannon Ridge Family of Wines, 90
Shed Horn Cellars, 92
Sol Rouge Winery, 98
Steele Wines, 100
Thorn Hill Vineyards, 104
Two Angels, 114

Petit Verdot
Aliénor Cellars, 110
Brassfield Estate Winery, 58
Fults Family Vineyards, 70
Hawk and Horse Vineyards, 74
Langtry Estate & Vineyards, 78
Obsidian Ridge, 113
Olof Cellars, 86
Shannon Ridge Family of Wines, 90
Shed Horn Cellars, 92
Six Sigma Ranch & Winery, 94
Steele Wines, 100

Pinot Blanc
Steele Wines, 100

Pinot Grigio
Thorn Hill Vineyards, 104

Pinot Gris
Brassfield Estate Winery, 58
Fults Family Vineyards, 70
Shannon Ridge Family of Wines, 90

Pinot Noir
Brassfield Estate Winery, 58
Fore Family Vineyards, 68
Gregory Graham Wines, 72
Kaz/Lakeport Winery, 76
Shannon Ridge Family of Wines, 90
Six Sigma Ranch & Winery, 94
Steele Wines, 100
Stonehouse Cellars, 102
Thorn Hill Vineyards, 104

Port/Port style
Don Angel Cellars, 66
Kaz/Lakeport Winery, 76
Six Sigma Ranch & Winery, 94
Primitivo Port
Kaz/Lakeport Winery, 76
Petite Sirah Port
Don Angel Cellars, 66
Langtry Estate & Vineyards, 78
Thorn Hill Vineyards, 104
Sauvignon Blanc Port
Kaz/Lakeport Winery, 76
Syrah Port
Kaz/Lakeport Winery, 76

Primitivo
Rosa d'Oro Vineyards, 88

Refosco
Rosa d'Oro Vineyards, 88

Riesling
Brassfield Estate Winery, 58
Chacewater Winery, 64
Steele Wines, 100
Wildhurst Vineyards, 106

Rosé (various varietals)
Boatique Winery, 56
Brassfield Estate Winery, 58
Cache Creek Vineyards, 62
Chacewater Winery, 64
Gregory Graham Wines, 72
Laujor Estate, 80
Mt. Konocti Winery, 82
Olof Cellars, 86
Rosa d'Oro Vineyards, 88
Shed Horn Cellars, 92
Smiling Dogs Ranch, 96
Stonehouse Cellars, 102

Roussanne
Steele Wines, 100

Sagrantino
Rosa d'Oro Vineyards, 88

Sangiovese
Don Angel Cellars, 66
Fults Family Vineyards, 70
Laujor Estate, 80
Rosa d'Oro Vineyards, 88

Sauvignon Blanc
Aliénor Cellars, 110
Art+Farm Wine, 111
Beaver Creek Vineyards, 54
Boatique Winery (Musquè), 56
Bodkin, 111
Brassfield Estate Winery, 58
Cache Creek Vineyards, 62
Chacewater Winery, 64
Dancing Crow Vineyards, 112
Don Angel Cellars, 66
Fults Family Vineyards, 70
Gregory Graham Wines, 72
Kaz/Lakeport Winery, 76
Langtry Estate & Vineyards, 78
Laujor Estate (Musquè), 80
Mt. Konocti Winery, 82
Noggle Vineyards & Winery, 84
Shannon Ridge Family of Wines, 90
Shed Horn Cellars, 92
Six Sigma Ranch & Winery, 94
Smiling Dogs Ranch, 96
Steele Wines, 100
Stonehouse Cellars, 102
Thorn Hill Vineyards, 104
Two Angels, 114
Wildhurst Vineyards, 106
Late Harvest Sauvignon Blanc
Aliénor Cellars, 110
Fore Family Vineyards, 68
Mt. Konocti Winery, 82
Late Harvest Sauv.Blanc/Sémillon
Thorn Hill Vineyards, 104

Sparkling Wines
Fults Family Vineyards, 70
Six Sigma Ranch & Winery, 94
Thorn Hill Vineyards, 104
Black Bubbles (Syrah)
Steele Wines, 100
Sparkling Pear Wine
Lady of the Lake, 115
Sparkling Nebbiolo
Olof Cellars, 86
Sparkling Sauvignon Blanc
Bodkin, 111

Syrah
Aliénor Cellars, 110
Brassfield Estate Winery, 58
Cache Creek Vineyards, 62
Chacewater Winery, 64
Fore Family Vineyards, 68
Gregory Graham Wines, 72
Kaz/Lakeport Winery, 76
Laujor Estate (Syrah Noir), 80
Mt. Konocti Winery, 82
Obsidian Ridge, 113
R Vineyards, 113
Shannon Ridge Family of Wines, 90
Shed Horn Cellars, 92
Six Sigma Ranch & Winery, 94
Smiling Dogs Ranch, 96
Sol Rouge Winery, 98
Steele Wines, 100
Wildhurst Vineyards, 106

Tempranillo
Brassfield Estate Winery, 58
Laujor Estate, 80
Mt. Konocti Winery,82
Six Sigma Ranch & Winery, 94
Smiling Dogs Ranch, 96
Steele Wines, 100
Tejada Vineyard Company, 114

Viognier
Gregory Graham Wines, 72
Langtry Estate & Vineyards, 78
Mt. Konocti Winery, 82
R Vineyards, 113
Steele Wines, 100

Zinfandel
Boatique Winery, 56
Brassfield Estate Winery, 58
Chacewater Winery, 64
Cougar's Leap, 112
Don Angel Cellars, 66
Gregory Graham Wines, 72
Kaz/Lakeport Winery, 76
Laujor Estate, 80
Mt. Konocti Winery, 82
R Vineyards (old vine), 113
Shed Horn Cellars, 92
Smiling Dogs Ranch, 96
Sol Rouge Winery, 98
Steele Wines, 100
Stonehouse Cellars, 102
Thorn Hill Vineyards (old vine), 104
Wildhurst Vineyards, 106

Farmers' Markets

For the growing numbers of people who want to shop locally, and eat fresh seasonal produce, the county has some excellent and well-supported Farmers' Markets. They are held in the summer months at a number of locations: Library Park, Lakeport (*Tues 10:30 am–2 pm May-Sept*), and Steele Winery, Kelseyville (*Sat 8:30–noon May-Oct*). There are plans for markets to open in other Lake County locations. For more information see: *www.lakecountyfarmersfinest.org* and *lakecountybewell.org*

LOCAL FARMS SELLING SEASONAL PRODUCE

Dancing Poly Farm
2550 Soda Bay Road,
Lakeport, 707-413-0054

Frontier Farm Co.
18525 S. State Hwy. 29
Middletown, 707-355-1001

Hanson Ranch
3360 Merritt Road,
Kelseyville

Leonardis Organics
1010 Argonaut Road,
Lakeport, 707-483-4004

Love Farms
1545 Scotts Valley Road,
Lakeport, 707-227-8647

McKay's Ranch
3125 Scotts Valley Road,
Lakeport, 707-263-7613

Renker Farms
2297 Argonaut Road,
Lakeport, 707-279-4409

Seely's Farm Stand
(Limited hours, call first)
Upper Lake, 707-275-0525

Artisanal Olive Oil

Lake County's Mediterranean climate, long-proven ideal for pears, walnuts and winegrapes, has a new contender for the limelight–olives. The county's artisanal olive producers are winning gold medals from major competitions (with world-wide entries). The range of olive varieties grown in the county almost equals that of winegrapes, with an array of exotic Italian, Greek and Spanish names. Emilio De la Cruz, the Master Miller at Chacewater Mill, can easily take his share of the glory, as he expertly mills many of the county's winning oils. The Chacewater Winery is a great place to sample his many creations such as the Meyer Lemon Olive Oil (*in process right*).

Organic Suppliers

Many of Lake County's first settlers bred livestock, and the ranching tradition is alive and well. The large expanses of open lands lend themselves to the growing demand for chemical-free, grass-fed meats. Six Sigma Winery & Ranch supplies grass-fed beef (*left*) and lamb as well as pastured pork. Many of the animals graze amongst the vines. Shannon Ranch also has grass-fed lamb. As well as the many farm stands and Farmers' Markets there are also some organizations who supply boxes of organic seasonal fruits and vegetables to your door or at drop-off points throughout the county. See *www.lakecountyorganicsplus.com*

Food Lovers' Lake County

The deeply agricultural nature of this county is evident everywhere. Each season has something spectacular from the pear orchards in blossom in spring, to the glorious fall vine colors, or the walnut trees turning bright yellow just before winter. The high quality of local organic fruit, nuts, vegetables, goat cheese, honey, and grass-fed animals is a magnet for foodies. Lake County Wine Studio offers regular food & wine pairing events, as do many wineries at special wine events. Wonderful farm-to-table dinners and harvest parties are hosted by many wineries in the Summer & Fall.

Dancing Poly Farm & Cooking School

Bess Giannakakis and Blaise Bahara have transformed a lovely old Big Valley barn, nestled among vineyards and olive trees, into a commercially licensed kitchen. This exciting venue is going to be "the hub of many wonderful gastronomic events." They also run an organic farm next to the school, where they grow a wealth of fruits, vegetables and herbs. This supplies fresh produce for the school, and for the two Farmers' Markets they attend nearby. Cooking classes are held from spring into late fall, and will cover topics such as: Knife Skills, Mediterranean Style, Canning, Homemade Pasta & 3 Sauces, Low & Slow: the Art of True BBQ, and French Sauces. Bess has been a professional chef and restaurateur for over 30 years, and has a passion to share her knowledge and love of good food. Dancing Poly also provides a catering service for private events. For more details visit *dancingpoly.com*

Lake Sport & Spectacle

For many in Lake County a good day out often involves spending time at the lake. With 100 miles of shoreline, and numerous docks and launching spots to choose from, every kind of water sport can easily be enjoyed. Throughout the year, starting with the opening of bass tournament season in January, there are many events that draw a big crowd. Not all events involve boats: there is an annual amphibious vehicle rally, where cars take to the lake, and a Sea Plane "Splash-In," where planes do the same.

Fishing Tournaments

Clear Lake is truly a world-class destination for fishermen. People from all over the US, and the world, are drawn to the sheer size and quantity of fish in the lake. There are at least 40-50 different catch-and-release tournaments each year. The *Clear Lake Bass Team Tournament,* organized by the Lake County Chamber of Commerce, brings over 100 fishing teams into the county to compete. No wonder—an average weight of 5 lbs. per fish is needed to win here—compared to 2 lbs. on most other lakes! Winners of the 28th event, Kelly and Kyle Maughs (*right*), caught over 65 lbs. of bass in 2 days. Crappie and Catfish are also excellent to fish. The *Clearlake Oaks/Glenhaven Catfish Derby* attracts well over 1,000 participants each year.

Wood & Glory

The Northern California Chapter of the *Antique and Classic Boat Society* will host their 20th "Wood & Glory" event on Clear Lake this year. It is indeed a glorious event as 50-60 of these classic wooden boats–more floating works of art–elegantly glide to numerous fun events held over a 4-day sojourn in the county. The boats come from all over the West Coast to compete and parade. The public can also vote for a *"People's Choice"* award. A final dinner at Boatique Winery is a very fitting last lap.

Sprint Boat Grand Prix

35 years ago, Clear Lake was "speed boat heaven," say organizers Rolf Kriken and Jack Long who have spear-headed the recent revival of this event, in close collaboration with city and county officials. The first 2-day event, in June 2017, saw a crowd of over 1,000 people come to watch these boats take off from Library Park (*right*). The 14 different events are sorted by class. The vintage racing class offers an exciting look at sprint boat history. Some of the modern boats can reach speeds of over 150 miles an hour–the lake's long course really lets the boats show what they can do!

Top left: Riders enjoy the sunset at Hawk and Horse Vineyards.

Top right: Rare vernal pool flowers at Boggs Lake Ecological Reserve.

Center: Redbud in bloom on the popular annual spring hike at the beautiful Brassfield Estate Winery.

Left: The spectacular cut-your-own Tulip Festival at Boatique Winery.

Top opposite: Mountain biking and off-roading are popular activities.

Center opposite: A fisherman and a kayaker leave Rodman Slough for the open waters of Clear Lake.

Opposite: A herd of magnificent Tule Elk near Cache Creek; bird watchers spot a Western Grebe.

Lake's Natural World

Lake County is a haven for outdoor pursuits, as there are 600,000 acres of public lands and well over a 100 miles of hiking trails to explore in the county, state, and national parks and forests. There is a network of trails and community pathways for hikers, cyclists, horseback riders, and paddlers of all abilities. Mountain biking and horseback riding are also popular local activities. Mendocino National Forest and South Cow Mountain offer authorized off-roading possibilities. Many of the state parks such as Clearlake State Park have camping facilities. There are also many private campgrounds for star-gazing and sleeping under the stars.

Lake County Quilt Trail

A truly delightful feature of local wine touring is the Lake County Quilt Trail, the first in California. 100 of these beautiful, brightly colored quilt squares adorn old barns and other notable landmarks across the county. Marilyn Holdenried, who organizes the county's annual Pear Festival, saw the quilt trail idea on a visit to Tennessee and thought it would be perfect for Lake County. She was so right–the idea has been warmly embraced by this small farming community. The volunteer team who make them (right) have difficulty keeping up with demand! Not only a joy to see, this soulful folk art tradition is a wonderful expression of local pride and spirit.

Above: The talented and enthusiastic creative team who make the quilt squares happen. Left to right: Gerri Groody, Carol Maxwell, Marsha Thibodeaux, Lyn Hilton, Marilyn Holdenried, and Annette Higday. "We resemble a quilting bee, but instead of fabric we have paint," says Marilyn Holdenried, the founder of the project. This impressive program of art in public spaces has captured the heart and soul of the community and visitors alike.

Photographer and journalist Karen Pavone, who was inspired to take all these pictures, was captivated by the project. "It was like a wonderful game of eye spy" to chance upon these squares. You can see more on her blog farministasfeast.com.

Wine Touring Resource Guide

WINERY ASSOCIATIONS

Lake County Winery Association

PO Box 1474
Kelseyville, CA 95451
(707) 357-5237
www.lakecountywineries.org
Association to promotes Lake County wines and wineries through events such as the Lake County Wine Adventure.

Lake County Winegrape Commission

3865 Main Street
Kelseyville, CA 95451
(707) 279-2633
www.lakecountywinegrape.org
Members organisation which promotes Lake County winegrape growers and runs the Master Vigneron program.

LIMOUSINE SERVICES

Dock Factory Lake Limos
(707) 263-0586
Lake County Limousine Service
(707) 263-5466
Limousine Connection
(707) 279-8889

TAXI/CAR SERVICES

Clearlake Cab Company
(707) 994-8294

Lake Co. Taxi
(707) 349-9903
(call or text) or email at:
lakecotaxi@gmail.com

Lake Co. Taxi Clearlake
(707) 994-3100

Maria's Midnight Rides
(707) 349-0446

Michelle Meese (Uber driver)
(707) 533-9676, 4 passengers

Riley's Cab Company
(707) 263-1690

TOURING SERVICES

Michael Van der Boon
(707) 260-2788
Local driver available for wine touring (can book by the hour)

Wine Country Touring and Tasting
(800) 692-8440 x 12
www.touringandtasting.com/
Wine-County-Tours
tours@touringandtasting.com
Company offering customized and flexible tours of wine country. Trip planning, reservations, and multi-county options.

VISITOR INFORMATION

Lake County Visitor Information

www.lakecounty.com (800) 525-3743
The county web site has good information about the very wide range of "things to do" in Lake County. The site also includes listings of where to eat and where to stay..

Lake County Chamber of Commerce

875 Lakeport Boulevard
Lakeport, PO Box 295, CA 95453
(707) 263-5092/(866) 525-3767
www.lakecochamber.com
The Chamber offers information on-line and at its office. They provide a monthly events calendar, brochures and fliers. They also produce *"Destinations"* a very useful visitors magazine which is a comprehensive guide to local activities and businesses.

STATE & COUNTY PARKS

Anderson Marsh State Historic Park

8400 Highway 53
Lower Lake, (707) 279-4293
www.parks.ca.gov
Nature walks, guided tours of park, and historic ranch house led by Anderson Marsh Interpretive Association (AMIA)
www.andersonmarsh.org
info@andersonmarsh.org
(707) 995-2658

Clear Lake State Park

5300 Soda Bay Road
Kelseyville, (707) 279-4293
www.clearlakestatepark.org
Email:friendsofclsp@gmail.com
Visitors Center, camping, picnicking, boat launch, fishing; Wild Flower Brunch in April.

Rodman Slough County Park

1005 Nice/Lucerne Cutoff Rd.
Lakeport (707) 262-1618
www.lakecounty.com/place/rodman-slough-county-park
Good spot to put a kayak in the lake and for bird watching.

NATURE PRESERVES

Rodman Preserve and Nature Education Center

6350 Westlake Road
Upper Lake, (707) 262-0707
Guided nature walks every Sat am; 8 am June-Aug, 9 am Sept-May
www.lakecountylandtrust.org
Rodman Explorer's Children's Nature Program for ages 7-12 is held Sat am April-Nov. Call for details.

Boggs Lake Ecological Reserve

Harrington Flat Road
Nr. Loch Lomond, (707) 262-0707
www.lakecountylandtrust.org
This is a fine example of a vernal pool, which are protected in California. It has an interpretive trail. Has wonderful rare flower shows in early spring. Good for birdwatching.

STATE & NATIONAL FORESTS

Boggs Mountain Demonstration State Forest

www.boggsmountain.net
Closed for public safety. Check website above for re-opening information.

Mendocino National Forest

Upper Lake Ranger District, (707) 275-2361
10025 Elk Mountain Road
www.fs.usda.gov/mendocino
260,000 acres of this vast forest are in Lake County. The Upper Lake Recreation Area (a short drive north of Upper Lake), has 355 miles of trails for hikers and horse riders, and 235 miles set aside for motorized off-road vehicles. There are many camp grounds maintained by Forest Service Rangers.

Cache Creek Wilderness

BLM Ukiah office (707) 498-4000
Highway 20 (8 miles east of Clearlake Oaks)
www.blm.gov/ca/ukiah/cachecreek.html
Trails are managed by the Bureau of Land Management. A great place for hiking and to see birds and Tule Elk. The BLM leads hikes to see Bald Eagles in winter.

GETTING OUT ON THE WATER

Eyes of the Wild
Wildlife & scenic pontoon boat tours.
(707) 262-2401 or (707) 349-0026
www.eyesofthewild.us
Birdwatching and photography tours.

Lake Guide Service
Shallow-bottomed boat ideal for fishing
and scenic tours of wetlands & birding.
www.lakeguideservice (707) 349-6178
Guided fly-fishing and birdwatching.

Ross England's Clear Lake Guide Service
5020 Steelhead Drive, Kelseyville,
(707) 349-1427
Fresh water bass fishing & coaching

Disney's Boat Rentals
401 South Main Street
Lakeport, (707) 263-0969
www.disneyswatersports.com
Rents boat for fishing, waterskiing, wake-
boarding, pontoon boats and jet skis.

Clear Lake State Park
5300 Soda Bay Road, Kelseyville,
(707) 279-4293
www.parks.ca.gov
Camping and cabins available to rent.
Marina with slips and boat launching.

The Lodge at Blue Lakes
5135 West Highway 20, Blue Lakes,
upper Lake (707) 275-2181
www.thelodgeatbluelakes.com
A wide range of watercraft for hire
including electric boats, kayaks, stand up
paddle boards and dockside fishing.

UP IN THE AIR

Lampson Field (local) Airport

600 Sky Park Road
Lakeport, (707) 263-2341
www.airnav.com/airport/1O2
Public airport 4 miles south of Lakeport.
General aviation airport with B-1 designation.

Aerial Archives

Herb Lingl, the Director of Aerial Archives,
lives in Lake County and creates custom
aerial photography from his own aircraft.
(415) 771-2555
aerialarchives.com/contact.htm
www.aerialarchives.com
Aerial photographs on pages 16,49,51 and
52 are from Aerial Archives' large library of
current and historical aerial photography.

OUTDOOR ACTIVITIES

For great information about how to enjoy
the 100,000s of acres of public access
lands, and explore the 100-mile perimeter
lake, KRT is an invaluable resouce. The
award-winning website has maps and
details of local hiking, cycling, paddling, and
horse riding trails, docent-led hikes to the
peak of Mt. Konocti, and other events.

Konocti Regional Trails (KRT)

For information on regional trails and
community pathways in Lake County,
contact info@konoctitrails.com or
(707) 263-2580, www.konoctitrails.com.

BIRD WATCHING

Lake County is a bird watchers paradise,
319 species of birds can be seen here.
The wide variety of habitats, with oak
woodlands, wilderness areas, lake,
marshes and an abundance of fish make
this a bird haven. Every season brings
new delights with Osprey, Eagles,
Pelicans, and nesting grebes being
some of the highlights.The county and
state parks are great for birding, and
some linked volunteer organisations
offer guided birding trips

Rodman Preserve & Nature Centre

6350 Westlake Road, Nice/Lucerne
Cutoff, Lakeport
lclt@lakecountylandtrust.org
(707)262-0707 or (707)994-2024
Lake County Land Trust leads a 1.5 mile
hike in this preserve adjacent to the
slough on Saturday mornings. Tuesday
visits also possible (check website)

Clearlake State Park Interpretive Association (CLSPIA) (707) 279-4395

www.clearlakestatepark.org

Anderson Marsh Interpretive Association (AMIA) (707)995-2658

www.andersonmarsh.org

Redbud Audubon Society Association (707) 263-8030

redbud.audubon@gmail.com

QUILTING SHOWS

Lake County's thriving quilting community
puts on some spectacular shows.

Annual Quilt & Fiber Arts Show

Lower Lake Schoolhouse Museum
16435 Morgan Valley Road
Lower Lake, (707) 995-3565

Falling Leaves Quilt Show

First Sat & Sun in October. Lake County
Fairgrounds, Lakeport, (415) 209-3044
www.llqg.org

SPECIAL INTEREST

Taylor Observatory & Norton Planetarium

5725 Oak Hills Lane, Kelseyville
Observatory Coordinator: (707) 262-4121
www.taylorobservatory.org
A research grade astronomy telescope.
In operation for 32 years – under a dome.
Planetarium shows.

Calpine Geothermal Visitor Center

15500 Central Park Road,
Middletown (707) 987-4270
www.geysers.com/visit
www.lakecochamber.com

Lakeport Auto Movies (Drive-In)

52 Soda Bay Road, Lakeport
(707) 263-5011
lakeportautomovies.paradisecinema.com.
One of the last remaining drive-ins,
featuring double-feature specials for
all ages during the summer.

Eleven Roses Ranch

5456 New Long Valley Ranch Road,
Clearlake Oaks, (707) 998-4471
www.elevenrosesranch.com
Day trips at historic family-owned working
ranch (from 1883). Wine tasting and hors
d'oeuvres. In Spring, take a mule-drawn
wagon on a wildflower tour.

©Nathan DeHart

Dancing Poly Cooking School

2550 Soda Bay Road (707) 413-0054
www.dancingpoly.com
A wide variety of cooking classes are
hosted at this lovely Big Valley farm
and culinary centre (see page 125).

LAKE COUNTY CASINOS

Konocti Vista Casino, Resort, Marina and RV Park

2755 Mission Rancheria Road,
Lakeport, (707) 262-1900
www.konocti-vista-casino.com

Robinson Rancheria Resort & Casino

1545 E. Highway 20, Nice,
(707) 275-9000 www.rrrc.com

Running Creek Casino

635 E. Highway 20,
Upper Lake, (707) 262-5500
www.runningcreekcasino.com

Twin Pine Casino

22223 Highway 29, Middletown,
(707) 987-0197
www.twinpine.com
Holds daily tastings in their *"Off the
Vine Tasting Room & Gift Shop"* plus a
Winery of the Month wine and food
pairing event. Sun-Thurs 10 am-9 pm;
Fri- Sat 10 am-10 pm.

GOLF COURSES

Adams Springs Golf Course

14347 Snead Court, off Highway 175,
Loch Lomond, (707) 928-9992
www.adamsspringsgolfcourse.com

Buckingham Golf & Country Club

2855 Eastlake Drive, Kelseyville,
Pro Shop (707) 279-4863
www.buckinghamgolf.net

Hidden Valley Lake Golf Course

19210 Hartmann Road,
Hidden Valley Lake (707) 987-3035
www.golfhvl.com

Riviera Hills Golf & Recreation Club

10200 Fairway Drive, Kelseyville
(707) 277-7575
www.rivierahills.com

BlackRock Golf Course

16451 Golf Road, Cobb,
Golf: (707) 928-9611
www.blackrockvenue.com

MUSEUMS

Lake County Historic Courthouse Museum

Open: 10 am-4 pm Wed-Sat; noon-4 pm
Sun255 North Main Street,
Lakeport, (707) 263-4555

Lower Lake Historic Schoolhouse Museum

Open: 11 am-4 pm Wed-Sat
16435 Main Street, Lower Lake,
(707) 995-3565

Ely Stage Stop & Country Museum

Open Sat-Sun, 11 am-3 pm
9921 Soda Bay Road (Highway 281),
Kelseyville, (707) 533-9990

Gibson Museum & Cultural Center

Open: Thur-Sat 12 pm-4 pm
21267 Calistoga Road, Middletown,
(707) 809-8009
http://cgibsonmuseum.com

PERFORMING ARTS

Lake County Symphony Orchestra

Soper-Reese Theatre (707) 263-0577
www.lakecountysymphonyassociation.org

Soper-Reese Community Theatre

275 South Main Street,
Lakeport, (707) 263-0577
www.soperreesetheatre.com

Concerts with Conversation

Tallman Hotel, 9550 Main Street,
Upper Lake, (707) 275-2244
www.tallmanhotel.com/concerts
Concert series in January-April. Acclaimed
musicians play informal concerts and
also interact with guests.

LIVE MUSIC

Monday Blues & Sunday Brunch

Blue Wing Saloon Restaurant, 9520 Main
St. Upper Lake, (707) 275-2233
www.tallmanhotel.com/weekly-music
Touring & local Blues bands every Monday
evening 6:30-9:00 pm. On Sundays in the
summer musicians play inside or outside in
the Tallman courtyard garden from 11 am.

Montain High Coffe & Books

Meadow Springs Shopping Center, Cobb,
(707) 928-0461, and at 18983 Hartmann
Rd., Hidden Valley (707) 987-8086
www.mountain highcafe.com
Popular spot for musicians and book lovers.

Smiling Dogs Ranch Tasting Room

Live music every Friday evening 6:30pm-
9:30pm. A popular venue for local musicians
to gather for a lively night of wine and music.
3955 Main Street, Kelseyville,
(707) 279-2762
www.smilingdogsranch.com

ART & GALLERIES

Lake County Arts Council & Main Street Gallery

325 North Main St., Lakeport,
(707) 263-6658
www.lakearts.org
First Friday Fling, a Monthly Reception
for artists showing in the Gallery with music,
hors d'oeuvres and wine tasting. Classes

Lake County Wine Studio

9505 Main Street, #1
Upper Lake, (707) 275-8030
Feb-Dec "Meet the Winemaker" & Artist
reception the first Friday, 5-8 pm and
Saturdays, 4-7 pm, each month. "Wine &
Art" classes 1st Saturday of month.

ART IN PUBLIC SPACES

Middletown Art Center & Garden

21456 Hwy 175, Middletown,
(707) 809-8118
Open Thur 11-4, Fri 11-6, Sat 10-6, Sun 11-4
New home of the EcoArts Lake County
Sculpture Walk Outdoor display of large-scale
sculptures, as well as many inside exhibitions

Lake County Quilt Trail (see p. 130)

www.lakecountyquilttrail.com
Beautiful quilt squares displayed on barns and
prominent buildings. Maps available at many
tasting rooms and online.

HISTORIC ACCOMMODATIONS

Lake County has a wide variety of places
to stay from camping in State Parks, to the
many Airbnb/VRBOs, or bed & breakfasts
and hotels. See the county Visitor Information web site. Below is a selection with a
particular historical or wine connection.

Tallman Hotel (see page 116 also)

9550 Main Street, Upper Lake,
(707) 275-2244, www.tallmanhotel.com
This 17-room historic hotel has an outdoor
garden courtyard for dining, live music, (and
a summer music festival). The Blue Wing
Saloon Restaurant serves local wines.

Suite On Main, Kelseyville

3965 Main Street, Kelseyville,
(707) 349-5682, www.suiteonmain.com
Situated in the heart of Historic Kelseyville,
this 1940's building has been completely
renovated into 5 very comfortable suites.
Each has its own kitchen and living area,
with unique & very stylish furnishings.

VINEYARD ACCOMMODATIONS

Crimson Hill Guest House at Gregory Graham Winery (VRBO 317086)

This 3BR/2BA guest house is situated in
a Red Hills vineyard. Large deck (with a hot
tub) has beautiful views over Anderson
Marsh. Sleeps 8. Dog-friendly/fenced yard.
Tour and tasting included. (707)-995-3500
www.airbnb.com/rooms/19606196

The Laujor Vineyard Loft (VRBO 606244)

A large 1BR/1BA (sleeps 4) loft apartment
with full kitchen) is above this Red Hills
area tasting room. Set in the vineyards with
spectacular views of vineyards, mountains
and lake. Complimentary wine tasting is
just downstairs. (707)-349-8236
www.airbnb.com/rooms/4660293

Bed & Barrel at Stone House Cellars

Agricultural Homestay and Bed and
Breakfast. Children welcome. Experience
winemaking or just enjoy simple country
peace and quiet. (707) 998-3378
info@stonehousecellars.com

Thorn Hill Vineyard Villa Suites

Three luxurious villa suites. Panoramic
views, complimentary continental breakfast, signature dark chocolate nightcap.
turn down service.(707)-279-2745
www.thornhillvineyardsbnb.com

Lake County Events Calendar

SPRING

Clear Lake Team Bass Tournament
MARCH
www.lakecochamber.com

Wildflower Tours
APRIL/MAY
www.elevenrosesranch.com

Wildflower Brunch
LATE APRIL
www.clearlakestatepark.org

Kelseyville Olive Festival
LATE APRIL
www.lakecounty.com

Heron Days
APRIL/MAY
www.redbudaudubon.org

Clearlake Oaks/Glenhaven Catfish Derby
MID MAY
www.clearlakeoaks.org/derby

Lake County Wine Adventure
LATE MAY
www.lakecountywineries.org

SUMMER

Lakeport Sprint Boat Grand Prix
JUNE
www.sprintboatgrandprix.com

Home Wine & Beer Makers Festival
JUNE
www.homewinemakersfestival.com

Middletown Days
MID JUNE
www.middletowndays.org

Independence Day Events/Fireworks
4TH JULY
www.lakecounty.com

Red, White & Blues
4TH JULY
www.lakecountywineries.org

Lake County Rodeo
EARLY JULY
www.lakecountyrodeo.com

Blue Wing Blues Festival
AUGUST
www.tallmanhotel.com

A Taste of Lake County
LATE AUGUST
www.lakecochamber.com

Lake County Fair
LATE AUGUST
www.lakecountyfair.com

FALL

Labor Day Blues Festival
LABOR DAY MONDAY
www.tallmanhotel.com

Clear Lake Seaplane Splash-In
SEPTEMBER
www.clearlakesplashin.com

Lake County Wine Auction
SEPTEMBER
www.winealliance.org

Kelseyville Pear Festival
LATE SEPTEMBER
www.kelseyvillepearfestival.com

Falling Leaves Quilt Show
EARLY OCTOBER
www.llqg.org

Konocti Challenge Bike Ride
EARLY OCTOBER
www.konoctichallenge.com

Oktoberfest
EARLY OCTOBER
www.lakecochamber.com/oktoberfest

Steele Wines Harvest Festival
MID OCTOBER
www.steelewines.com

WINTER

Christmas In The County
EARLY DECEMBER
www.visitkelseyville.com

Sparkle Party Lake County Wine Studio
DECEMBER
www.lakecountywinestudio.com

Lake County Symphony Christmas Celebration
DECEMBER
www.lakecountysymphonyassociation.org

Concerts with Conversation
JANUARY-APRIL
www.tallmanhotel.com/concerts

Guided Bald Eagle Tours
JANUARY- FEBRUARY
www.ca.blm.gov/ukiah

Barrels & Verticals
FEBRUARY-MARCH
www.lakecountywineries.org

Wine & Chocolate
MID MARCH
www.mtkonoctiwines.com/www.lakefrc.org

Guided Nature Walks
ALL YEAR
www.lakecountylandtrust.org

To contact the publisher email: gaye@meadowlarkpublishing.com